C000243656

GROOMING FOR GINNY

Grooming for Ginny

ELAINE PICKWORTH

Foreword by Virginia Leng, MBE

THRESHOLD BOOKS

First published in Great Britain by
Threshold Books, The Kenilworth Press Ltd,
661 Fulham Road,
London SW6 5PZ
1989

British Library Cataloguing in Publication Data
Pickworth, Elaine
Grooming for Ginny.
1. Livestock : Horses. Grooming
I. Title
636.1'083

ISBN 0–901366–86–2

Typeset by Rapid Communications Ltd,
London WC1
Printed in Great Britain by
Biddles Ltd Guildford and King's Lynn

Contents

Foreword

by Virginia Leng, MBE

I was very touched when Elaine asked me to write the foreword to her first book, which, judging by its contents, will not be her last. It is full of information, excitement, sensitivity and charm I hope you will enjoy reading it as much as I have.

Elaine has been one of our family for many years: not only has she been invaluable as a 'groom' but also as a dear friend. She has helped us through the ups and downs of our challenging sport. Her knowledge regarding training young horses and travelling with international event horses is considerable. I know that any young hopeful will gain valuable information and encouragement from reading this book.

Virginia Leng

Preface

I consider it a privilege to have spent the greater part of the last five years working with Virginia Leng (formerly Holgate) and the wonderful horses in her Ivyleaze yard. During this time I have tried to absorb as much knowledge as possible, in an effort to discover what makes a good event yard tick. During my stay I have been fortunate to be part of a team whose exceptional rider has managed to progress from being a Burghley winner to a Badminton winner, a European champion, a world champion and an Olympic bronze and silver medallist.

Over the years I have kept a diary of my activities and have drawn on my notes to write this book, which highlights some of the more memorable experiences of those five years. I have tried, in addition, to include details of some of the more practical aspects of event-yard management so that readers will be able to employ some of the Ivyleaze methods with their own horses and riding. I hope, too, that I have provided more than a glimpse behind the scenes of one of the foremost eventing yards in the world.

Elaine Pickworth
May, 1989

Acknowledgements

I would like to thank everyone who has helped me with the writing of this book, especially Heather Holgate and Virginia Leng, who first suggested that the idea was possible.

I am also grateful to all those kind people behind the scenes who have offered ideas on how subjects could be tackled or improved.

To Lesley Gowers I owe great thanks for her patience and advice while editing the manuscript.

PICTURE CREDITS

Elaine Pickworth – 16, 23 (bottom), 28, 31, 37, 40, 62, 65, 75, 81, 85, 105, 112, 116, 123, 126

Kit Houghton – 15, 19, 23 (top), 27, 47, 66, 69, 73, 74, 79 (top), 101, 119, 138

Paul Jeremiah – 35, 39, 43, 51, 56, 59

Wendy Tyrrell – 93, 96, 99

Barn Owl Associates – 130, 133, 136

John Birt – 109

Christopher Fear – 111

CHAPTER I

In at the Deep End

I set off for my interview at Ivyleaze just a few days before Christmas in 1983. I was driven from my home in Hexham, Northumberland, down to Avon by Dawn Broughall, an instructor friend who had suggested that I would benefit from the experience of becoming a working pupil in a top competition yard.

I spent the long journey trying to imagine what I would be asked, whether I would be up to the job and whether they would even be remotely interested in offering me a place. The hours passed almost as quickly as the scenery.

After leaving the motorway at the wrong junction, we eventually arrived at the yard via the scenic route. Ivyleaze is situated just a few miles from the hallowed ground of Badminton Park, the very heart of three-day eventing, and I knew that this was very horsey country indeed. The rider I was hoping to work for was Virginia Holgate, then an up-and-coming event rider who, just three months earlier, had won the Burghley horse trials with her talented horse, Priceless.

I was to be interviewed by the two people who had most influenced Ginny's career and helped her to achieve her success: her mother, Heather Holgate, and her trainer, Dorothy Willis. Dot, apparently, is an old friend of Dawn Broughall's – hence the introduction. The interview was to include a kind of 'trial run', which would last three days.

It seemed natural that I would end up working with horses. I had started riding at a very early age and my family on my father's side had enjoyed a long association with horses. As

13

a young man my grandfather had ploughed the land with Shires, and it was he who brought my sister's first riding pony, whom I later took over.

I had served my time with the local Pony Club – the South Northumberland – and had passed my Pony Club 'B' test. I had ridden various horses in the past and felt confident that I could handle most of them. Later I discovered I had much to learn.

As we approached Ivyleaze I could see horses out in the two paddocks in front of the house. The house itself was white-washed, though slightly grey in places, and was perched on a small rise. It was quite exposed, there being few trees around to offer shelter. The drive, about a hundred yards long, led to a few outbuildings. From the road no one would have guessed that these buildings enclosed such a busy yard.

We were greeted by a large, ferocious-looking Rottweiler, who was the yard's guard-dog and took her job seriously – up to a point. Dawn jumped out of the car and brushed her aside; I gave her a somewhat wider berth as she padded up to sniff the car.

We were greeted by Mrs Holgate, who was very smartly dressed – from her appearance you would never have guessed that she worked with horses. She took us into the kitchen of the house to explain the drill and mentioned that Ginny was away and wouldn't be back before I departed. I was disappointed not to meet her – after all, she could have been a dragon for all I knew.

The kitchen was beautifully decorated; in fact the whole house was very pretty and tastefully furnished throughout.

Since we had arrived in the evening we were treated to supper. I ate mine in the kitchen with the other grooms, who had come in to dine and watch the TV there. This gave me my first opportunity to chat to Maria and Siobhen, both of whom had worked on the yard for some time. Dawn ate with Dot and Heather in the room they called the study.

Dawn and I were to stay with Dorothy and Siobhen in the cottage about a hundred yards down the drive. Maria lived in the attic of the main house.

After my long journey and all the excitement of the day I had no trouble falling asleep – and I knew I would have an early start the next day.

I was up at 6.30 am and out on the yard at 6.45 to help give the horses their first feed. Then we started on the mucking out and hung the horses' hay outside their stables so that they could be given a little at a time during the day. I tried to fit in where I could and had to keep asking Maria what I should do next. When we had finished morning stables we had breakfast in the cottage.

As was usual, Heather had prepared a list of the day's proceedings and tasks, with notes as to which horses were to be turned out and when, and which horses were to be exercised and by whom. I was due to ride Streaker, a grey Thoroughbred gelding who was about seven years old and who, I was informed, had a nasty temper.

Dot was out on the yard most of the time. She was quite an imposing figure and I kept my distance, not daring to say much at all.

The two paddocks in front of the house at Ivyleaze. In the foreground Priceless is enjoying a roll.

Two Ivyleaze residents gossiping in the field.

I had to ride Streaker in the Holgates' manège, in front of Heather and Dot. I wanted to show them that I was a good rider and did my best to get him on the bit and going well.

Streaker was a horse that Ginny had evented up to Intermediate level, but a nasty fall had caused her to lose her confidence in him. He was relegated to the role of school horse and was perfect for the job because he would only go as well as he was ridden.

Dorothy decided that we should tackle a few fences. At this point Streaker and I discovered that we had very different ideas about where we should take off. How I stayed on board I'm not sure – perhaps my pride held me in place. More than once I saw the floor looming toward me. I don't think that anyone was too impressed with my jumping style – but at least I showed that I knew how to stick on.

There were fewer horses in the yard than I had expected. In addition to Streaker I was introduced to Sandy, Puff, and two youngsters – Quiz, a yearling, and Hovis, only eight months old. There was also Ben, a three-year-old who had just been broken in. The 'big boys' (as they called the more experienced eventers) were away on their holidays (out at grass on a nearby farm) and would be coming back in to work at the beginning of the year.

I had the impression that things were rather relaxed, with Christmas only a few days away. In the afternoons we cleaned the tack, strapped off the horses and got them ready to go out or stay in. Depending on whose turn it was, someone had to go up to the house at around 4.30 pm to help Heather with the evening meal. This left the others to feed and carry out the last checks.

In our less busy moments I was able to ask the others about Ginny. I had to know what she was like to work with, although from what I had seen and heard she was thoroughly charming and likeable. Unanimously she was given a glowing reference, so, reassured, I had no further worries on that score.

In the evenings the grooms were left very much to their own devices, although someone had to check the horses at 6.30 pm to see that they were warm enough and to give them more hay. Later, at 9 pm, we had to skip them out, check their water, give them hay and/or a fourth feed, and make sure that they were comfortable for the night.

While I was there the weather wasn't too brilliant and I vividly remember sliding around in a muddy rain-soaked paddock, trying to skip it out after the horses had been out in it overnight.

I was allowed to hack out on Sandy, who was a very sweet-natured individual. I was quite shocked to discover that another working pupil had fallen off him and broken her leg – hence the reason for the vacancy.

The yard had just one manège, which was outdoors and used come hail or shine. It had a Dormit surface and seemed to ride well. Heather explained that the value in having an outdoor arena lay in the fact that the horses had to learn to perform in all weathers. This meant that when they were asked to do a test in a howling gale or torrential rain they would not be distracted by it. Though an indoor school undoubtedly is more convenient from the rider's point of view, I could see the wisdom of Heather's remarks.

The yard itself consisted of ten boxes, all facing inwards on to a sort of quadrangle. The tack room flanked one side of the oblong. The hay racks in the older boxes were fixed quite high on the walls and when I first filled them I tended to get a mass of hay seeds down my neck. In the end my aim improved so much that I could throw the hay up while standing back – I probably would have made a good goalshooter in a netball squad!

On the third day, Heather and Dot took me on one side and told me that they would be willing to take me on as a working pupil. I felt really honoured that they thought me good enough. Although I had only been with them for a few days I couldn't help but be impressed with the way the yard was run and with the attention to detail that was paid to the horses' welfare. I was in a quandary, however. Making the decision left me with a slight headache as to what to do with my own animals at home. I promised to let Heather know in a few days.

Mission accomplished, Dawn and I set off for home and merged into streams of traffic heading for the Christmas holidays.

I had four horses at home, all of which would have to be found places to go to or be sold. One, a mare, was in foal so she would have to stay, no matter what.

After talking things over with my mum, who neither pushed nor influenced, I decided to give up the course I was studying at college – it hadn't lived up to expectations anyway – and sell two of my horses.

Advertisements were placed in the local paper, and on New Year's day someone came to look at my youngster and subsequently bought her. The youngster's mother was lent to some friends who wanted to buy her in the spring when the necessary capital would be available. That left our broodmare and my 14.2 hh pony, whom Dawn was going to hunt.

Hovis, ready to welcome visitors to the yard.

The money I received for my youngster paid for my first year at Ivyleaze.

On 11 January, I packed my bags and set off for the South. I travelled down by train via Newcastle and Bristol, to Bath, where I was met by Maita, an American who was working at Ivyleaze as a secretary. I'm afraid she couldn't have thought me a very good travelling companion – I hardly said a word. I was suddenly overwhelmed by the fact that I had left home to begin a new phase in my life.

I arrived at Ivyleaze to discover that Siobhen had taken to her bed and could not work on the yard. An old injury to her foot hadn't mended correctly and had started to cause her great pain. It looked doubtful that she would be able to stay on, which meant we would be one short. On top of this I learned that Maria was to leave in three weeks' time as she was coming to the end of her year as a working pupil. I realised that I would soon have the yard to myself, a prospect I found rather daunting – and I had only a few weeks in which to learn the ropes. I began to understand the meaning of the phrase, 'in at the deep end'.

The big boys – Priceless, Night Cap and Murphy Himself – were back and raring to go. Ginny, too, had returned from her holiday. When I first met her she was schooling Priceless in the arena.

Ginny's riding was both stylish and quiet. She seemed to be doing very little yet Priceless was purring along, beautifully balanced and on the bit. As she moved him effortlessly round the school her legs never left his side, and her hands were tactful and giving.

Dot introduced me as Ginny cantered past. I managed to squawk a feeble greeting and, somewhat dumb-struck, I stood and watched.

I'm not sure what I had expected but she seemed quite normal and didn't have two heads.

20

CHAPTER 2

The Ivyleaze Team

O ne of the major factors contributing to Ginny's remarkable success over the years has been her back-up team,
Ginny herself will often compare her role to that of a Grand
Prix racing driver, saying that without her team of 'mechanics'
her 'car' wouldn't be in tip-top condition to produce the
goods. The highest priority on the yard is the horses' health
and welfare, that way they have the best possible chance of
performing well.

Everyone at Ivyleaze has to pull together, whatever they
are doing, and it is important that relationships are good,
both between the girls on the yard and between them and,
say, Heather or Ginny. If, for any reason, someone is not
pulling her weight or not trying her best, the link in the chain
is broken.

At Ivyleaze everyone lives at very close quarters, which
means you get to know one another pretty well – for better
or worse – and there are times when you need to find your
own square inch of space in which to breathe. At times ideas
do conflict, and sometimes you have to weigh up the advan-
tages of tackling a job another way. Often, though, the tried
and tested methods still prove the best.

When I first arrived at Ivyleaze, just sixteen and still wet
behind the ears, I used to see Ginny on the yard most days.
More recently business in London has kept her away a fair
bit. As a rule, Ginny doesn't do much of the hacking – that is
Heather's forte. We normally leave a couple of horses behind
for Ginny to school while we take out the first ride. Usually it

is two of the novice horses, unless Ginny wants to school the advanced horses first.

Very occasionally Ginny will take one of the horses out for a hack. One morning Heather and I were hacking sedately from Acton Turville to Badminton when we were suddenly passed by Ginny and Priceless, cantering along the grass verge at a rate of knots and jumping all the drainage channels. Heather's face was a picture, and she turned to me and said, 'Now you know why she doesn't do the hacking.' Many top riders find hacking boring and can only suffer it if they liven it up. On Ginny's hacks, walk is an unheard-of pace.

Ginny does all the fast work herself although one of the grooms will often accompany her on another horse. She gives us instructions as to which bits the horses are to use so that we can adjust the tack in advance.

Ginny is very strict with the horses when they are in the school. They are there to work and when they go well and try hard, even if they find it difficult, she always rewards them with Polo mints and pats. During the season Ginny is out in the manège all morning, schooling and jumping the advanced horses, or bringing on the novices.

Spending so much time in the saddle undoubtedly contributes to Ginny's fitness, but she also finds time to do some skipping in the evenings. Running is definitely out, though I have seen Ginny jogging a couple of times. She once asked if she could borrow a pair of my boots, and I lent her my brand new pair of black leather jodhpur boots. Some time later I spotted her coming back from jogging, still wearing my best new boots!

More recently Ginny has taken to working out on an exercise bike, too, pedalling away like fury in front of the TV or to pop music at full volume.

I have never ceased to be amazed at how Ginny manages to ride and compete on big strong event horses after her dreadful accident in 1975 when she broke her left arm in no less than twenty-three places. She was riding a horse called Jason VI at the time, and when he hit the deck she pushed her arm out in front of herself to break her fall. The arm under-

Ginny in action with Master Craftsman at the Vicarage Vee, Badminton, 1989.

Ginny modelling her new 'made-to-measure' hat!

went a four-hour operation, after which the news was not good. The surgeon, Commander Bertram, feared that the nerves were so badly damaged that Ginny would never recover full use of that arm. He decided to operate once more to re-assemble some of the shattered bones. A second opinion, sought by Ginny and Heather, confirmed that the surgeon had done a brilliant job.

Three more operations later Ginny still had very little feeling in the arm. It took eight frustrating weeks of waiting and hoping before she felt a sensation of tingling in her fingers. After that, things improved slowly, and day by day, Ginny gave herself new tasks to build up strength and mobility.

But the arm was still not right as Ginny couldn't straighten it fully. During a routine visit to Ivyleaze, Don Attenburrow, the yard vet, looked at Ginny's x-rays. After studying them closely he suggested ways of straightening and strengthening the arm. His advice was to prove invaluable.

Today Ginny's left arm is by no means as strong as the right. Her strength comes from her shoulder, which she uses to great effect to compensate for the weakness in the lower limb.

Ginny never forgets how lucky she is and is thankful that she found such an outstanding surgeon. Whenever the subject is brought up she plays down the injury and her subsequent achievement. Her injury is trivial, she says, compared with a lot of others that people suffer.

With Ginny's obvious fitness and stamina I was quite surprised to discover that she smoked. In fact, one of the sure signs that she is under pressure is the number of cigarettes she gets through in a day – no doubt they help her to find a few minutes' relaxation in her ultra-busy schedule. Two of the most important items I have to carry with me at competitions are a packet of cigarettes and a box of matches. Many are the times I have been sent hot foot to the lorry to fetch them, so I know now not to forget them.

One of the more comical episodes relating to Ginny's smoking involved two new Irish horses that Ginny and I went to fetch straight off the ferry at Fishguard. The horses had undergone a long and arduous journey by the time they arrived at their new quarters at Ivyleaze. Having given them a few hours to settle in and recover, Ginny thought she ought to ride them. She mounted the first one and no sooner had she got her foot in the stirrup than he took off down the arena, bucking all the way. Ginny just about managed to stay on board and pulled him up. I was surprised to see that she still had a cigarette sticking out of the corner of her mouth – though it was rather squashed. She decided to lunge the other horse before it was ridden.

During the afternoons Ginny usually has plenty of correspondence to catch up on, which means that she is always on hand if we need to ask her advice. In fact, Heather, Ginny and Dot never mind being asked questions, no matter how trivial or daft, because doing so usually avoids a mistake.

Finding time to relax in a hectic life is difficult for all of us involved in the Ivyleaze team, but this is especially true for Ginny. Even at night the phone never stops ringing, largely because people know they have a better chance of catching her in.

Ginny has been a great help with my riding, though on the whole she lets Dot teach the working pupils and tends not to get involved. On one occasion I was riding a horse called Bally, a grey horse on whom I was hoping to compete, and was having difficulty in getting him on the bit. Dot and Heather were at a loss as to how to help me. The more I tried, the more he refused to co-operate, and I was blocking him unwittingly through my actions. Ginny, who had been preoccupied with another matter, came to the rescue. She made me work in a circle around her and barked instructions at me. If there's one thing I hate it's being shouted at, but something clicked and when Ginny stopped shouting I realised that the horse was in the correct outline, yet I didn't seem to have done anything to achieve it. Perhaps I had been trying too hard to do everything right instead of just letting it happen. Later, the same thing occurred with a horse called Noddy. Once again Ginny bawled at me and, although I resented being yelled at, it had the desired effect.

Ginny often refers to me now as her 'nanny'. To be honest, I quite often *feel* like a nanny, checking to see that she has done what she is supposed to do and making sure that she has everything she needs. Apart from the cigarette supply mentioned earlier, I also have to keep a special eye on her 'lucky' whip, which she has a habit of dropping somewhere near the end of the cross-country course at major events. It is her very favourite stick and it goes with her to all the big competitions. I even had to have it repaired, which probably cost more than a replacement, but we couldn't just buy a new one.

As a rule Ginny bandages her own horses at competitions, even the novices. Gradually, as I improved, I was allowed to bandage the novices and was thrilled at Witton Castle in 1988 to be asked to bandage two advanced horses, Master Craftsman and Beneficial. I was nervous while they did their cross-country rounds, willing the bandages to stay put. Ginny said I was the only person ever to put on the front protectors for her, and I was pleased that I would know what to do if Ginny is delayed at a competition.

Ginny will quite often discuss the horses' way of going with me and, no matter how busy, will always make time for a chat. Sometimes she will ask me to watch her jump so that I can tell her, for example, how well a horse is picking up its front legs. At Gatcombe once, Ginny talked through her reasons for not running a horse, asking me what I thought. I expect she had already made up her mind – but it was nice to be asked.

When I first went to Ivyleaze it was quite a wrench to leave home and all the security I had enjoyed there. Heather was very good in helping me to adapt to my new life and its responsibilities. She tried to get to know my moods and helped me work things out generally. She never forgets that the road to success is a difficult one, and recognises that staying at the top can be even more difficult because so much is expected of you.

I admire her principles of stable management, and whilst others may dismiss her approach as fussy, they must surely realise that her attention to detail pays dividends. I've often heard Heather say that nothing comes for free in this life, and never was a truer word spoken when it comes to producing top competition horses.

Heather is quite a strict person and always straight to the point, so you know where you stand. If you've done something wrong you learn how to put it right, and in the end your own competence and efficiency improve. Heather's standards are very high and maintained at all times, at home and in public.

Heather is responsible for buying most of the young horses, although Dot and Ginny have to be in agreement as well. It's no good buying a brilliant horse if Ginny won't ride it. However, if Ginny had had her way Master Craftsman would have been sold on as a five-year-old. Heather, who had done most of his early schooling herself, insisted that he had the talent and the ability to make it to the top, and a dubious Ginny reluctantly agreed to keep him on.

One of the most important qualities to look for in an event horse is a good temperament. If a horse has all the ability in the world but refuses to work with you, you might as well give up. Or, if a horse is too excitable or highly strung, he might just explode when you need it least – in the dressage arena. Today, horse trials can be won or lost in the dressage phase; it's not enough that horses jump brilliantly across country and over show jumps.

Heather with Con, a youngster from Ireland.

Grooming for Ginny

Basic conformation has to be correct, and good style over fences is also sought. Of course, you can never guarantee how far a horse will go, but with correct training he can be given every chance. The Holgate system has been proved to work, time and again.

Dot Willis, who oversees the yard and the training, has been an indispensable member of the Ivyleaze team since 1981. Before that she was head girl to Pat Manning, a trainer who has helped Ginny tremendously over the years. Like Heather, Dot is a perfectionist and everything she does is given her full attention at all times.

When I first arrived at Ivyleaze I tried so hard to do my work well that I spent more time chasing my tail and as a result didn't do anything properly. To begin with I had a total memory lapse about putting the lids back on the feed bins, a habit which drove Dot to distraction. One night I was tucked up in bed after evening stables when Dot, checking the yard last thing, discovered my error. Although there was a wall between us I heard every word that was uttered. My name was mud. Frequently I would lie in bed wondering if I had

Dot, in conversation with Priceless.

remembered to put the lids in place – and dreading the out-
come if I hadn't.

Dot is as strict with the horses as she is with the yard staff.
If the horses are naughty they are corrected. She never allows
youngsters to get away with little tricks, because she knows
that they will develop into nasty habits later on.

Dot usually gives her lessons in the afternoon, and they
take place whatever the weather. Often I am invited to watch
a lesson, particularly if Dot wants to drive home a point.

Another important member of the Ivyleaze team is Heather's vet, Don Attenburrow, who has a practice outside
Exeter. When the Holgates lived in Devon, Don was their
vet and they've kept him ever since.

I find it fascinating to watch Don work, and he always
takes the trouble to explain what he is doing as he goes
along. Sometimes the horses are taken to his practice for
treatment, and there he is in his element, surrounded by
complicated pieces of equipment and employing the very
latest techniques.

Over the years Don has worked wonders with the Ivyleaze
horses and if it wasn't for him I doubt that Priceless would
be alive today. In 1982 Priceless contracted leptospirosis
and there were times when no one thought he would pull
through. However, due to massive doses of TLC (tender lov-
ing care) and Don's close supervision, he rallied round, once
again showing the courage of the little fighter that he is.

If a horse is suspected of being unwell, we ring Don and
give him as much information over the phone as we can.
He will ask questions about pulse and respiration rates, the
horse's food and water intake, whether or not it has passed
droppings, etc. If after this verbal examination he feels it
necessary to see an animal, he comes to the yard himself.

All the working pupils take a pride in knowing intimately
each horse they look after. If a horse doesn't quite seem
himself he will be monitored closely for a few days and his
condition discussed with the vet. Ivyleaze never takes chances
with its horses' health.

During my stay we haven't had many emergency calls, but

if ever a horse requires urgent attention the local vet is called in, thereafter to liaise with Don.

Robert Hall, who comes from the Malmesbury area, is the yard farrier. He usually manages to cheer us all up on his afternoon visits. Coffee is a must and if ever we forget or are busy, he never fails to remind us of the importance of keeping the farrier happy, saying things like, 'No foot, no horse'.

We try to get as much wear out of a set of shoes as possible, but the amount of roadwork we do plays havoc with the shoe metal. At one time all the horses wore road studs behind for hacking, but we decided that they weren't good for their legs as they contributed to nasty wind galls, which reduced again once the studs were removed.

Studs and stud holes are the bane of our lives. Often grit lodges in the holes or damages the stud threads. We put one stud hole in each shoe: behind they are placed near the end of the outside of the shoe, and in front they are placed in the middle of the outside edge.

If the ground is very hard, the horses are fitted with pads under the shoes. The novices use Unitex pads, which are easy to deal with and have proved a great success. The big boys use chrome-leather pads pre-soaked in oil to make them supple and to help them mould to the shape of the foot. All the pads have the frog area cut out so that they don't interfere with the frog action. This also allows the pads to fit more snugly and helps to prevent the shoe being ripped off easily. We have to take care that no dirt or grit finds its way between the pad and the foot, and in some cases we successfully avoid this by packing the frog area with cotton wool.

Generally, Robert cuts back the horses' feet so that they are quite short and there is no extra strain on the tendons, and he shoes them hot to ensure a good fit. Road nails are fitted in front to afford a better grip on the slippery road surfaces around Acton Turville.

The working pupils vary in age, but Heather prefers to employ yard staff straight from school so that they don't have too many preconceived ideas about how things should be done. During my time there, quite a few pupils have come

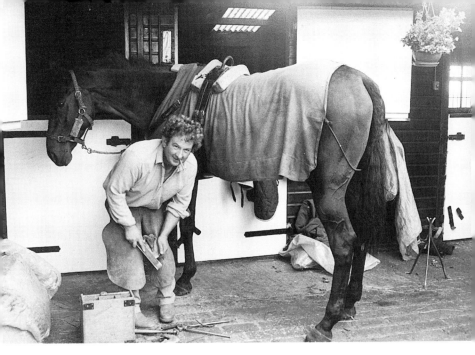

Robert Hall, the yard's farrier, at work.

and gone, some staying longer than others. Normally there are three or four of us to share the workload for about ten horses.

When I first went to Ivyleaze the gardens were lovingly tended by a splendid local character called Bob. For some inexplicable reason he decided that I was Welsh and insisted on calling me 'Taffy'. It was a wonder I didn't suffer an identity crisis as Don has always maintained that I am Irish! Doesn't anyone recognise a Geordie accent these days?

CHAPTER 3

The Ivyleaze Horses

During my five years at Ivyleaze I have been lucky enough to work with a number of different horses. Some stayed on to make the grade, others were just passing through, learning the ropes on the way. This chapter is devoted to the horses with whom I had the most contact and to those whose character and temperament made them special.

When I first arrived at Ivyleaze, I was given three horses to look after: Priceless (known as 'P.'), Night Cap ('N.'), and a big bay horse called Titch. All three were totally different in size, shape and temperament.

P. was a very self-assured, independent little bay, standing just 16 hh. He had one white sock behind, which was the only white on his body. What he lacked in height he more than made up for in presence. He always gave the impression that he could look after himself and needed no one's help, thank you very much. However, as time went by we got to know one another pretty well and P. would look out for me in the yard and especially at three-day events.

He could be quite a grumpy individual in his box and disliked the whole process of grooming. He showed his disapproval by fidgeting, gnashing his teeth, and kicking out. Gradually I discovered that the best way to deal with this was to stand close to him, and when he moved, to move with him. Otherwise if I found myself stranded in the middle of the box, I became an easy target. Actually I don't think he ever meant any harm, because if he did make contact he was shocked and apologetic. Once, he caught me on the shin with a cow kick, so I was always a little wary of his back end.

Underneath his gruff expression he was soft as butter, and he adored being the centre of attention. Often, first thing in the morning while I was mucking out, he would breathe down my back and neck. If I ignored him he would gently tug at my shirt or jodhpurs. Never once did he nip my skin.

He could be quite a rascal when it came to being caught in the field, and once or twice Dot even had trouble catching him in his stable! Whenever he was turned out he always wore a headcollar, which helped a little, but on countless occasions I had to pad round the field behind him while he played his special version of tag.

When P. was five Heather decided to sell him, along with one or two others. Buyers came to look at him and someone agreed to take him. However, as luck would have it, he failed the vet!

To look at P. on his holidays during the winter in his thick woolly coat, it was hard to believe that he was indeed a world-class event horse. Someone once joked that they'd give Ginny £1000 for her hunter!

In the autumn of 1984 P. was brought in from the field with a nasty kick on the inside of his forearm. It was duly poulticed and, although a small bump remained, it caused no further problem. A few weeks later Ginny took him to the Horse of the Year Show to make an appearance in a parade of Olympic medallists and for some fun in a celebrity jumping competition. While she was warming up for the latter, P. stopped at one of the practice fences. This worried Ginny, as P. *never* stopped at his fences – it was quite out of character for him. She re-presented him at the jump, and he popped over it obligingly. In the actual competition he jumped a good clear – but the outing left a nagging doubt in Ginny's mind.

When Don came to the yard on a routine matter a week or two later, Ginny asked him to look at P.'s leg. He x-rayed the lump and told Heather not to turn P. out until he gave the all clear. The x-ray revealed a hairline fracture. If P. had been hunted or if he had turned awkwardly on the leg, the bone could have snapped at any time. The consequences didn't bear thinking about.

Don gave us strict instructions about P.'s enforced stable rest. For the next three months I had to walk him out in hand for some grass four times a day to keep him occupied. He was a little terror sometimes – more than once we didn't get as far as the grass because he started to play around. I would then turn him round and take him straight back to his stable, from where he would watch my every move, sullenly. Needless to say, the next time I took him out he was as good as gold. He was a quick learner.

During this time we had to put him on a diet to prevent him putting on too much weight. He didn't think much of this idea and protested by banging loudly on his stable door. He discovered that Heather was a bit of a soft touch where he was concerned and would bang twice as loudly whenever she appeared on the yard. He knew she would take pity on him and give him a large handful of hay.

Thanks to Don's expert care and advice, P. recovered fully and the next year regained his earlier form. The rest of his career is eventing history and his story has already been told in Ginny's book, *Priceless* (published by Threshold Books).

In 1986 P. was retired to the hunting field, where he is still having a great time in the expert hands of Louise Bates, MFH to the Pytchley.

In contrast to P., Night Cap was a very trusting fellow and a real gent who would never dream of doing anything naughty. He was a dark brown gelding who stood 16.3 hh and had a small white star on his forehead. He was by the same sire as Priceless – Ben Faerie – and was foaled in the same year.

N. suffered slightly from always living in P.'s shadow. In another yard he would have been number one without a doubt. In 1985 his one-day record was brilliant – he won every competition he entered. At Badminton the same year he was third while P. was first.

If anything, N. was a shade unlucky, often sustaining a

Night Cap and Ginny competing at Gatcombe in 1986. When Priceless retired at the end of 1986, N. moved into the spotlight.

knock before an event, which kept him out of the competition. Heather always felt he missed out a little as a youngster.

He was a sensitive soul, much more so than P. or Murphy. N.'s finely tuned antennae would pick up his rider's tension, especially at a big competition. Sometimes it was more than he could take, and he would boil over and be silly.

When P. retired at the end of 1986, N. moved into the spotlight. With the yard's attention focussed on him, he responded by taking on a more positive role. He became a little cheeky, too, helping himself to brooms or haynets left near his stable door and waving them triumphantly for all to see.

N. was the type of horse who needed outings before a major competition to help him settle and relax. Just before the European Championships in 1987 we took him up to Thirlestane Castle in Scotland so that he could practise his dressage and show jumping in the atmosphere of a big competition. While he was warming up for the jumping he was clearly distracted by a nearby brass band. Ginny was doing all the work and N. was hardly listening. Dot told Ginny not to look after him so much, with the result that he clouted the next fence he jumped. After that, he woke up and jumped clear.

Nicky Ide-Smith (known as 'Nicks'), a working pupil with whom I shared many happy times at Ivyleaze, got on really well with N. and often looked after him at competitions at home and abroad. There was a little friendly rivalry between us, as each of us wanted 'our' horse to win and to look the smartest – but it was all good fun and it kept our standards high.

Night Cap has also retired to the hunting field with Louise Bates – and he loves every minute of it. Louise must have the two finest hunters in the land.

Titch, a bay gelding, was a giant of a horse, measuring about 17.2 hh. Heather had bought him for schooling and selling on. He had come over from Ireland with a lorry-load of horses and I don't think Heather had originally intended to buy him, but she took him as well as another she wanted.

His show name was Hitchhiker: when he arrived he was covered with lice, or 'hitchhikers' as someone aptly put it at the time.

During my first year at Ivyleaze I rode Titch quite often. Heather smiles when she remembers the time I had an altercation with him when out on a hack. We were heading towards Badminton Park and Heather decided that we should go through an area of woodland. I was leading the way and came to a gate. I was about to open it when Titch thought he had a better plan. Why bother with a gate when you can simply barge through the hedge? Heather watched helpless with laughter as I disappeared through the bushes, Titch crossing his jaw to shut out my requests to stop. We emerged the other side covered in twigs and branches, like a pair of soldiers in camouflage.

Titch was responsible for landing me in hot water on more than one occasion. One summer, after Heather had just finished decorating the yard with hanging baskets, I was busily attempting to mount Titch when he suddenly shot forward, showering plants and potting compost everywhere. He was so tall that as I swung my leg over the saddle, I kicked one of the precious baskets, which in turn swung back and whacked him on the bottom. I was not in Heather's best books that day.

Titch was an odd sort of character and we didn't always get on. He never bothered to tell me when I was out of favour and would often surprise me by his behaviour. One day, when I was strapping him as usual, standing quietly at his shoulder, I suddenly found myself flying through the air

Murphy Himself at the end of his winter holiday.

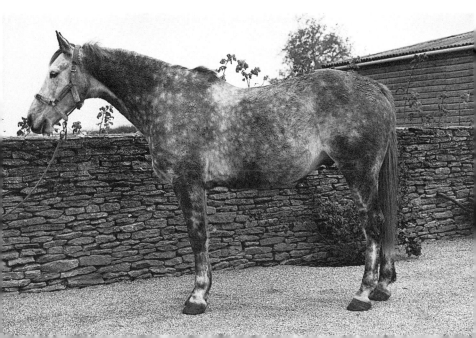

and heading for the stable wall. Quite without warning, Titch had picked me up by the scruff of the neck and tossed me to one side.

Murphy Himself was very much the up-and-coming star when I arrived at Ivyleaze. Although Heather is responsible for most of the horse-buying at the yard, Murphy was the result of one of Ginny's shopping expeditions.

A large grey horse standing every inch of 16.2 hh, he was bred in Ireland by a stallion called Royal Renown. Bought as a four-year-old, he was later discovered to be a year younger, a fact that was confirmed when Heather visited the stud where he was bred.

At times he was quite a handful to cope with and tended to take the law into his own hands. At one of his early events, in the middle of the cross-country, Ginny pulled the bit straight through his mouth in her efforts to turn him, and she had to dismount and put it right before continuing.

He liked to poke his head out of his stable door and then pull the most dreadful faces at passers by. If you dared to approach, he would bob his head up and down threateningly.

He pretended to hate being made a fuss of, but as soon as he was away from the yard he would whicker whenever he saw anyone he knew. At home, if you ignored the face-pulling, and bothered to talk to him he would stand for ages enjoying the conversation.

His wicked sense of humour was never more apparent than when you wanted to catch him in the field. He would saunter over to you, all sweetness and light, devour the nuts you had brought to tempt him, then wheel round and trot off, kicking his heels. Sometimes he would circle you in trot, just out of reach. I often thought he just wanted to test out my boredom threshold.

Whenever I rode him he always gave me a tremendous feeling of power, although he could be quite naughty in walk and would often shorten his stride. In my first year at Ivyleaze I

Murphy looking fit and well as he waits to set off on the cross-country course at Burghley in 1986. To everyone's surprise, he won.

remember cantering him along an airstrip, behind Ginny. She decided to jump a ditch and I followed her over. Murphy took it with ease, giving me a most wonderful feeling. Later that night, in the kitchen, Ginny said that it was the first time she had seen me smile for months. I must have been home-sick at the time.

Murphy proved his brilliance by winning Burghley in 1986, which was quite unexpected. However, in 1988, after reluctantly agreeing that Murphy was just too strong for her, Ginny swapped him for Griffin, a horse belonging to Ian Stark. As I write both horses are making great progress with their new owners.

Sambo was another character I had to look after. He was a Welton horse by Welton Louis. In looks he was very similar

39

Ben (right) and Master Craftsman, now the best of friends.

to P., being bay with a white sock and about 16.1 hh. He had lovely paces and was capable of doing a really good dressage test. He was also brilliant across country, but show jumping was his weak link.

Dot lunged him over poles and fences to try to improve matters. He would clear them with ease, and he seldom rattled a pole. However, as soon as he had a rider on his back it was a different matter. Whether he didn't like taking off quite where Ginny put him, we'll never know.

He was a sweet horse in the stable and had a delightful temperament. He was sold on to the States as an Intermediate and has been competing with some success over there.

Beneficial was one of three youngsters whom Heather was bringing on in 1984. The other two were Bally McGinty and Master Craftsman.

Ben, as Beneficial is known, is a cheeky little busybody who has to poke his nose into everything that is going on.

He is by Ben Faerie, the sire of P. and N., and he shares a lot of P.'s characteristics.

Often when he is turned out in one of the two front paddocks he will jump over the fence to join some companions on the other side. Sometimes he does it just for the change of scenery.

In 1985 Ginny and Ben were involved in a nasty accident at Smith's Lawn. The pulling-up area at the end of the cross-country had been effectively blocked off on one side by groups of spectators with children. On seeing them Ginny turned sharply in the opposite direction. Unfortunately, a tractor that had been working on the polo pitches was parked right in her path. With nowhere left to run, Ginny and Ben plunged into the ropes, Ginny somersaulting on to the adjacent road and Ben crashing on to his knees.

Ginny was taken to hospital and found to have fractured her wrist. Ben had damaged his knees so badly that we feared the joints might have been affected. Luckily they weren't, but the ugly wounds took months of patient care and attention to heal. To keep an even tension on his knees and prevent them from swelling we were advised to encase them in Tubi-grip bandages. The Tubi-grip worked well but had to be held in place with Elastoplast, which pulled the hair out. Today his knees are fine but he has a lot of white hair where the sticky tape was!

During 1987, when Ginny had rather a lot of horses to contend with, event rider Mandy Hosp took over the ride on Ben to further his education. They were seldom unplaced.

In 1988 he went to the Seoul Olympics as Ginny's second horse, but didn't have the chance to run. He knew he was there to do something, apart from biting the other horses and escaping from his box – but perhaps that was just his way of telling us he was bored.

Master Craftsman is another of Heather's highly successful purchases. She brought him as a four-year-old in the spring of 1984 from a Mr Spencer, a breeder from the Bristol area. She had taken Mark Todd with her to ride him, as Ginny was away that day. (Mark had been competing on a couple of Heather's horses at the time.)

Crafty is a Thoroughbred by Master Spiritus, out of a mare called Scalped who had raced. He had been bred for 'chasing but hadn't quite made the grade.

As a youngster he was a big, gangly, brown gelding standing 16.3 hh. We used to hope that he wouldn't grow any more. He has a very cool temperament for a Thoroughbred and takes everything in his stride. He has a sweet nature but I thought that he lacked a little character in his youth, although I doubt Heather would agree. Later, the more I came to know him, the more I began to like him.

He can be quite aggressive with the other horses when out in the field. On one occasion he decided to attack Ben and took off after him, galloping flat out, with his ears laid right back and his teeth bared. Ben, realising that discretion was the better part of valour, neatly departed from the field over the hedge and disappeared down the drive. Nowadays the two are inseparable, having flown halfway round the world together to Seoul.

When he first came he was desperately unbalanced and Dot spent a lot of time and effort lungeing him over trotting poles and cantering him on small circles. Sometimes she would put me on board when lungeing. He felt horrible – he would lean in so much that my inside foot was only a little way off the ground!

At first Ginny wasn't the least bit interested in him. She rode him only because Heather insisted that she should. At one stage Ginny wanted to swap him for another horse, or to sell him – but Heather's faith in him won through. Gradually, by earning her respect and proving his capabilities, he found his way into Ginny's affections too.

Being a relaxed character, he is relatively easy to look after. He rarely makes a fuss when introduced to something new. However, he did take exception to a fluffy sheepskin noseband that Ginny tried on him before a three-day event in Sweden. He entered the arena and practically did a headstand trying to rub it off with his front legs.

Another thing he doesn't like is flags – or anything flapping in a breeze, including his own slipped rugs!

Before Crafty went to the Olympics he had only competed in three other three-day events. The first was at Intermediate level in France, where he was fourth; the second was at Stockholm, where he was second; and the third was Badminton, where he was third. All things considered, the bronze and silver medals he brought home from Seoul were quite a remarkable achievement for a horse of his experience.

A quiet moment with Crafty at Badminton, 1989. The more I came to know him, the more I began to like him.

CHAPTER 4

The Challenge of Badminton

People often ask me what it's like to groom at Badminton. My first attempt (described in Chapter 7) was not a great success, but the following account of the 1988 competition may serve to answer this question.

The Badminton Horse Trials are the highlight of the spring season. A sort of eventers' Mecca, every year they attract hundreds of thousands of faithful devotees who come to watch the world's best horses complete for the Whitbread Trophy.

The Park in which the event is held makes a most wonderful setting, and living, as we did, just a few miles down the road, we could watch the annual preparations in progress. Gradually the stands are erected, scaffolding bridges appear, and arenas are marked out – and all these things are guaranteed to make our horses shy as they routinely hack through the Park in the early months of the year.

In 1988 Ginny had two horses heading for Badminton: Master Craftsman and Murphy Himself. Their competitive build-up included horse trials at Kings Somborne, Belton, Brigstock and Brockenhurst, with some extra dressage and show jumping at Bicton.

Ginny's first real indicator that Crafty was ready to tackle his first Badminton came at Kings Somborne. He went brilliantly round the open course, eating up the difficult fences with relish. Ginny was specially impressed with the way he executed the bounce into water, which had been worrying her. (Ginny used to have a bit of a phobia about bounce fences, and although she now launches into them without a care in the world, I don't think they could be said to be her favourite type of fence.)

As Ginny was weighing in after the cross-country, Heather asked with a smile if she would still like to sell him. Ginny had to agree that in this instance 'mother knew best'.

Murphy went well in the new Citation bridle which we had acquired. This was Murphy's first outing for a year and everyone was watching to see if Ginny had him under control. When he came down a steep hill in a collected canter the world could see, and so could Murphy, that he had met his match (at least, on that day).

The weekend before Badminton, while Ginny and her two hopefuls were at Bicton practising their dressage and show-jumping technique, I got stuck into the business of packing. Basically you have to cater for the horses' every need and I always resort to a checklist that I made some years ago. For the two horses I took the following:

2 dressage bridles
   rolled reins
   flash nosebands
   cavesson nosebands
   bridoon bits
   vulcanite D ring
   rubber D eggbutt snaffle
   French link
Double bridle
Murphy's Citation bridle +
   normal cross-country bridle
   as a spare
Crafty's cross-country bridle,
   cross-noseband + spare bridle
Spare set of cross-country reins
2 cross-country bags containing
   leg protectors + spare set,
   bandages + spares, over-reach
   boots + spares and extra-large
   5-strap Woof boots
2 breastplates and spare martingale attachments + spares

2 sets cross-country girths +
   spares
2 racing surcingles + spares
2 white dressage girths
2 dressage saddle cloths + spare
2 show jumping numnahs +
   spare
2 blue Cottage Craft girths
Brown and blue weight cloth
   numnahs
Weight cloth + spare lead
   (various sizes)
2 'every day' blue numnahs +
   girths
2 'every day' dressage numnahs
Spare set of shoes each
2 sheepskin nosebands (flash
   and cavesson)
Kieffer dressage saddle
3 jumping saddles (2 Barnsby's,
   1 Stübben)
Heather's black saddle

Lungeing cavesson and side reins
Lunge whip
'Every day' cantering gear – protectors, over-reach boots, bandages
'Every day' Woof boots
2 sets half Woofs for show jumping
Various spare bits (in fact the whole bit tray!)
Best headcollars and ropes + spare rope without clip
Nylon headcollar for washing down
2 Lavenham rugs
2 towelling rugs
2 smart sweat rugs
2 Thermatex rugs
Sponsor's rugs –
   2 woollen day rugs
   2 coolers
   2 long-neck rain sheets
Anti-cast rollers
Show rollers
2 exercise sheets
Water buckets
2 dustbins (for soaking hay)
Dustbin for equipment in the 10-minute halt box
Haynets/Horsehage net's
3 bales hay
Large bag chaff

2 bags Horsehage
7 scoops grass nuts/sugar-beet
1½ bags oats
1 bag event nuts
1 bag complete nuts
Minerals/glucose
Scales
Gloves
Broom
Skip
Fork
Buckets to soak sugar-beet etc.
Vet box – spare Fybagee, Vetrap bandages etc.
Plaiting box
Stud box
Cross-country and dressage whips
Ear muffs
Grooming kit – incl. tail bandages, mane things
Sponges
Sweat scraper
Kaolin – wraps, brown paper, etc.
10 pkts Animalintex
Towels (lots)
Everyday stable bandages and wraps
Fairy liquid
Wool fat and rubber gloves
Cotton wool and Gamgee
2 saddle covers

All this equipment had to be loaded into trunks etc., and taken over to Badminton in readiness for our arrival.

In 1988 we were stabled under the clock tower in the yard next to the house, and were lucky enough to have a spare stable in which we could keep all our belongings.

Ginny and Anna, another working pupil, hacked the horses over at about 11 a.m. on the Tuesday morning. They had to

Inside the old servants' hall at Badminton – our canteen for the duration of the three-day event.

take with them the horses' passports, as a vet checks the horses' vaccination records as they arrive and also their ID, just to make sure that the competitor has brought the right horse. Crafty's papers caused a bit of confusion as his passport showed little to identify him. In the end the problem was sorted out and he was admitted into the grounds.

By the time Ginny arrived at the stables, I had made the beds and tidied up generally. I fed the horses so that they would have time to digest their lunch before their lesson with dressage trainer Pat Manning.

I took my gear up to the grooms' accommodation above the stables. I have to say that the beds which are provided leave a little to be desired, and often you have to try a few before finding one which has hollows in the right places for you. I usually end up lying on top of my sleeping bag to soften the impact.

After their lessons in the afternoon the horses broke out in a cold sweat, so I kept a close eye on them. The stables provided are indoors, and the temperature inside tends to fluctuate – at times they are warm and stuffy; at others, decidedly chilly.

Other competitors and their horses were arriving and I looked out for faces that I knew. Nicky Flemming, who was grooming for Tanya Longson and Pink Fizz, popped in to say hello. She had a soft spot for Crafty ever since she had looked after him for a spell at Ivyleaze when training as a working pupil for a year.

On Wednesday morning I was up at 4.30 so that I could have the horses fed by five o'clock in readiness for an early jumping session with Ginny. I mucked them out, soaked the hays and curled up for a quick nap under some horse blankets next to the trunk, only to be disturbed forty-five minutes later by a patrolling policeman. Security in the yard at Badminton is tight, especially at night.

At about 7 a.m. I took the boys hacking in the Park, then Ginny schooled and jumped them. Murphy, clumsy clown that he is, managed to knock his splint, and although it wasn't tender, I poulticed it to be on the safe side.

Later I took the horses out for a graze in hand. They were used to being turned out daily and I knew they would miss their usual ration of grass.

After lunch I plaited up in readiness for the official vets' inspection at five o'clock. Ginny decided to work Crafty while I prepared Murphy and she didn't bring him back until 4.40 p.m., which meant I had just twenty minutes in which to make him look respectable.

On these occasions it is the done thing to present the horses looking immaculate – manes must be plaited, coats glossy, feet oiled, tails washed and brushed, etc. We always put on quarter markers to show off the horses' rumps, which we apply with a damp body brush and a stencil (they can also be done with a small comb). Boots are worn in case the horses play around on the way to the vetting, but are removed at the last minute; and I always check the horse's feet just before they trot up to make sure that there are no stones or gravel wedged in them.

Ginny likes to run them up in a bridle and reins, rather than a show bridle and chain, as the reins and bit give more control if a horse starts messing around. Also, she can more effectively straighten the horse's head and neck if he decides to admire the view when trotting up.

From a competitor's point of view the vetting must be the least popular part of any three-day event. So much depends on trotting up the horse correctly. If a horse is run up a little too fast, or too slow, his action can be affected, making him appear unlevel; or it may give the impression that the runner has something to hide. It is therefore crucial that each competitor knows exactly how to trot up his horse, and at the right speed. Keeping the horse's head and neck straight is another factor that can make a difference, as if the weight is carried more over one leg than another, a false picture can be presented.

The vets' inspection takes place in front of Badminton House. The gravel forecourt is swept back to expose the underlying tarmac, thereby providing a smooth, level surface. There are usually three members of the ground jury and one vet presiding, and it is a very serious affair.

With the vetting over, and my two still in the competition, I returned to the stables to unplait them and let them relax with their tea and haynets. I cleaned their bridles and put up the tack ready for Crafty's dressage test the next day.

On Thursday morning I had a lie-in until 6.15, then fed and mucked out the horses before going to breakfast. We grooms have all our meals provided at Badminton through the generosity of the event's sponsors, as is the case at most three-day events. The catering at Badminton is especially good so it's worth making the effort to attend at the stipulated times. The meals are eaten in what was once the servants' hall, next to the kitchens of Badminton House. The walls are decorated with stags' antlers and gleaming copper pots, pans and moulds, which must take a good deal of cleaning. Riders and owners can also use the facilities there, although they don't all receive meal tickets like we do.

After breakfast I returned to plait up Crafty. For dressage he has as many plaits in his mane as I can fit in, which is usually between eighteen and twenty-two. I brushed him off and tidied up his tail, which was full of shavings from his bed. Crafty's tail was so thin that I didn't dare brush it. Instead I had to pick out all the shavings by hand. However, it is our practice to use tail gloss to help prevent tangles – and this certainly makes the job easier.

Ginny arrived at 9 o'clock to take Crafty up to the working-in area near the main grandstand. His test was at 11.40 a.m. Ginny schooled him in Heather's black saddle, as the dressage saddle was a bit low and she didn't want to risk rubbing his back. I went up to watch Ginny ride and took a headcollar with me so that, if given the chance, Crafty could be grazed in hand.

Crafty seemed relaxed and was working well, so Ginny gave him a break before his test. I changed his saddle, smartened him up and left him with Dot, who stood and grazed him. Ginny and I went back to the stables and, while Ginny changed, I tacked up Murphy. I was to ride him up to the grandstand area to acquaint him with the sights and sounds thereabouts. I would be able to watch Ginny's test from my elevated viewpoint – on his back.

Pat Manning was there to help Ginny with some last-minute advice, and Crafty looked to be going well as he went into the arena. I could see that he was really trying hard to do his best, and from the illuminated marks going up above the three judges' boxes it was clear that I wasn't the only one who thought so. His mark was 54.4, which left him in second place behind Ian Stark's Glenburnie at the end of the first day.

Ginny was delighted with him, and so was I. We walked the horses away from the crowds, unplaited Crafty and allowed him to graze. Ginny then turned her attention to the business of schooling Murphy, who before she got on board, was looking thoroughly bored with the whole affair. From Ginny's point of view, this couldn't have been better.

Back at the stables I strapped the horses, fed them, cleaned the tack, made up suppers and left hay, sugar-beet and grass meal soaking. Having set the horses fair for the night I disappeared for a shower and food. Feeling human again, I joined a group of grooms catching up on the latest eventing gossip.

Ginny and Crafty having a breather before their dressage test. Badminton, 1988.

Friday was Murphy's day for dressage. His test wasn't until 3.50 p.m., which meant I could take things in a fairly leisurely fashion. Ginny wanted Murphy plaited up for his work, and she arrived at 10 a.m. to school him. I watched him being schooled in the Park for a while before fetching Crafty so that Ginny could take him for a canter. Ginny swapped horses and I took Murphy back for his lunch.

Some time later Crafty arrived, rather het up and still raring to go. Ginny complained that he had practically pulled her arms out. He must have thought he was doing the cross-country today. Perhaps he'd got his dates muddled up!

He was too hot to eat his feed so I led him out to the Park to graze and to help him settle.

Murphy went off for his test at 2.50 p.m. and looked good all the while that Ginny was working him in. He was still going well when he did his test – that is, until near the end, when he decided he'd had enough of this dressage lark and put on a more entertaining show for his audience. We were all a little disappointed with him, but Murphy looked quite pleased with himself!

Priceless, ready to make a few celebrity appearances to help raise funds for the Olympic appeal, arrived with Fran, his groom, and Louise Bates in tow (literally). He was sharing our corner of the stable block, in an adjacent box. We discussed the organiser's plans for him and discovered that he was supposed to be out in the Park while the cross-country was taking place. We all agreed that this was not a sensible idea – without a doubt Priceless would have joined in if he could. It was decided that he should be safely locked away in the stable during the afternoon.

That evening I walked the course with Fran and just about made it back in time for supper.

Later, I prepared the tack and equipment for the big day. I made up what we call the 'steeplechase bucket', which I have with me at the start of Phase A, and which I take up to the start of Phase B, the steeplechase. In it I put the following items:

Bandages and Gamgee	Lead rope
Saddle soap and sponge	Leather punch
Spare bridle and reins	Scissors, needle and cotton
Spare stirrup leather and irons	Spare surcingle
Cotton wool	Spare breastplate
Stud spanner and studs	Hoof pick (to put in my pocket)
Clean sponge and towel	Spare lead for weighing in at
Spare shoes with studs already	start of Phase A
in them	

Sometimes it is sensible to take a rug, too, because if it's raining or very cold, the rug can be thrown over the horse's quarters while he waits at the start of Phase B.

I also prepared the dustbin of equipment needed for the ten-minute halt box, as follows:

Badminton programme with	Glucose drink (for the horses)
course plan	Towels

2 buckets (for water)	New Zealand*
Sponges	Rider's coat
Sweat scraper	Drink for rider
Vaseline or wool fat and rubber gloves	Cigarettes and matches
	Headcollar and rope
Anti-sweat rug	Spare over-reach boots
Woollen day rug*	* Possibly one with steeplechase kit

The list may look small, but when it is coupled with the contents of the steeplechase bucket, we can usually cater for most eventualities.

Saturday morning dawned fair. I was up at about 5 to feed the horses and muck out.

After breakfast I plaited up both my horses, putting in fewer plaits than for the dressage. Crafty, who was running first, was given a second feed at 8.40, after which he was taken for a leg-stretch in hand.

Heather arrived at the stables to help get everything organised. She always sews the bandages in place after Ginny has put them on. She likes to allow plenty of time for this, as she hates having to rush the job. While I was helping to prepare Crafty, Dot took Murphy out for a walk in hand then gave him his second feed, at about 10.30 a.m.

In a spare moment Heather and I took our dustbin of kit up to the ten-minute halt box and found a safe place where we could leave it.

Anna arrived to bolster the support team. She had cycled from Ivyleaze on her rusty old bike to avoid the huge traffic queues waiting to enter the Park. A near miss with a bumper and a swerve into a brick wall told her that her brakes no longer worked!

By the time she appeared, Crafty was bridled, bandaged and booted. As usual we had looped a bootlace round the bridle headpiece and tied it to the first plait to prevent bridle and horse parting company in the event of a fall. On checking my watch, we had just twenty-four minutes before Crafty was to set off on the first set of roads and tracks, Phase A.

We walked to the start, near the house, and Ginny went off to weigh in. Crafty was obviously feeling fit and well. Every time we passed the starting box he bucked and plunged at a banner. He just couldn't wait to get going. A minute before the off, Ginny was legged into the saddle and counted down. With a flurry of the lead rope, Crafty was away.

We nipped over to the start of the steeplechase to wait for Ginny's arrival. Ginny smiled as she rode past and I knew all was well.

Crafty's steeplechase round looked fast but effortless, and, although he had been a little strong, Ginny was thrilled with him. When he'd finished I checked his shoes and bandages before sending him off on the second roads and tracks of Phase C. (There is a special 'dead' area designated for this.)

I picked up my steeplechase bucket and accepted a lift from Heather and her brother, Uncle Jack, to the ten-minute halt box. Anna, meanwhile, dashed off to the stables to give Murphy a leg stretch and to stitch on his back boots.

Fran and Louise, also pressed into service, met us in the box and we waited until Crafty and Ginny, threading their way through the milling spectators, appeared on the scene.

Before entering the box Crafty was trotted up in front of a vet, who checked him for soundness and signs of distress. Once given the OK, I took Crafty from Ginny and the back-up team went into action. I undid his noseband, making a mental note of which hole it was on, and loosened his surcingle and girth. His mouth was sponged out, and his neck was lightly sponged (we don't use a lot of water unless it is very hot). The saddle was raised and the saddle area rubbed vigorously with a towel to help the circulation and to dry off some of the sweat. His head was also rubbed around the ears. Heather gave him a glucose drink while I checked his shoes and studs.

I donned a pair of rubber gloves and began to apply liberal amounts of thick, sticky, wool fat to Crafty's forearms, knees and bandages, and smeared a little on his pasterns. I took care not to apply the grease so high that it could touch the reins and make them slippery. On his hind legs I greased from his stifles to his hocks, and down over his boots and pasterns. I also put a little on the backs of his fetlocks.

Once all these tasks had been accomplished, a rug was thrown over Crafty and I walked him round until Ginny was ready to get back on board. Meanwhile, Ginny was hearing from Dot and Louise about how earlier competitors had tackled the difficult fences and how the course was riding generally.

Five minutes before he was due to start, Heather called Ginny over and we tightened Crafty's girths and noseband. As is customary in the box, Ginny was given a leg up by Heather. She trotted Crafty round for a minute to check that she was happy with the stirrup length. We tightened the girths again, then Ginny walked to the start box to be counted down by the starter.

Crafty left the start box like a bat out of hell, releasing some of his pent-up enthusiasm. By the first fence he was under control. I watched until he was out of sight.

Once on their way, the support crew ran into the nearest tent to watch Ginny's round on the TV monitor. Crafty was on the cross-country at the same time as Ian Stark on Glenburnie, so we saw snatches of both rounds. Crafty was going brilliantly and was tackling the fences like a pro, though this was only his third three-day event. He came through the finish with plenty of running left in him but was just outside the time. More importantly, he was clear.

I rushed into action once more. Ginny had to weigh in before I was allowed to touch the horse. I found her favourite whip, which as usual she had dropped near the finish, then was permitted to take a hot and steamy Crafty. Ginny was whisked away by a TV interviewer; I could hear her singing Crafty's praises.

I untacked him, draped a sweat rug over him and led him back to the stables in his headcollar. I headed straight for the special washroom, where hot water is available on tap. First I gave him a general wash down with warm water to rinse away all the sweat and grime. I followed this with a wash down with cold water to help cool his body temperature. His bandages and boots were removed, carefully watching for any new bumps or scrapes. Then, using first a

Murphy waits outside the main arena, absorbing the atmosphere, while Crafty performs his dressage test. Badminton, 1988.

blunt knife then Fairy liquid, I removed the wool fat from his legs.

At this point Dot arrived to take over from me so that I could help Heather prepare Murphy for his onslaught on Badminton. I tacked him up while Heather sewed his front bandages in place. In a spare moment I zipped over to Crafty to poultice his legs and bandage him up. Normally we use Animalintex poultices after the cross-country but Ginny had specifically asked for kaolin. To save time, the night before I had spread the kaolin on pieces of brown paper cut to size, so all I had to do was bandage the poultices in place.

Ginny, meanwhile, was recovering in the lorry, no doubt smoking a cigarette or two.

At the appointed time, Murphy was taken up to the start of Phase A. Ginny appeared and asked me where her short whip was. I had left it in the usual place, the cross-country bag, and Dot volunteered to fetch it. A few minutes later she came back empty-handed. I couldn't understand it – I knew that it was there in the morning. Once Ginny was on board I dashed back to the stables and rummaged through the bag's contents. Right at the bottom I found the missing whip. I ran back to the start triumphantly. On my way there I was stopped by a friend who gave me a shamrock. As Murphy moved off on Phase A I hoped it would bring us some of that famous Irish luck.

Murphy was wearing his Citation bridle again, and it would be interesting to see how he went in the steeplechase. As expected, he went brilliantly and Ginny even wondered if the bridle was too severe as he was hardly pulling. I told her I thought she'd better wait until after the cross-country before she decided.

When Murphy arrived in the box for his 'pit stop', we carried out our usual routine. All seemed to be in order, and before long Ginny was counted down and the pair disappeared on to the course.

Once again, we all dived into the tent to watch the monitor. Murphy was going beautifully. Moreover, Ginny looked totally in control as they flew over fence after fence. Murphy jumped the lake complex faultlessly and boldly, hardly batting an eyelid ... then the monitor suddenly interrupted Ginny's round to show another competitor. Unable to stand the suspense I ran outside hoping that I could see something from the box. A gasp went up from the crowd. I struggled back into the tent to see Ginny sitting on the ground hugging her leg, unable to get up. She had fallen at the bottom of the ski jump.

Where was Murphy?

I gathered my wits and ran outside to find him. He appeared to be galloping amongst the spectators. I shouted to Heather not to worry about the horse as I would see to him.

Fran and I headed off in the direction of the ski jump. One of the officials had caught Murphy, which made my task easier. Heather and Dot went off to find Ginny, while I led Murphy back to the stables. There wasn't a mark on him, so I didn't think he had fallen. I later discovered that in his keenness to get on with the job he had totally ignored Ginny's requests to pop over the log at the top of the ski jump, and had put in an enormous leap over it instead. In so doing he had launched poor Ginny straight out of the saddle. Lucinda Green had had exactly the same problem with Willy B.

'So much for the shamrock', I thought.

As we made our way through the crowd, people kept asking me if Ginny was all right. They were genuinely concerned about her welfare.

Murphy, the rascal, was still full of himself and wanted to know if he could complete the course. I told him I wasn't speaking to him so he pranced, jogged, barged and spooked all the way to the stables.

I washed him down and checked him over. He was absolutely fine. Ginny, meanwhile, had gone off for x-rays.

Having made Murphy comfortable, I took Crafty (now sporting a halo) out for a leg-stretch and bite of grass. I had to walk him for ten minutes on the hour until Heather and Dot had checked him last thing at night.

Murphy also went for a stroll and a graze and showed no apparent stiffness whatsoever. We were disappointed that he hadn't completed the course, but it was no good harping on about it. Crafty had gone brilliantly and now needed our full attention.

Ginny's x-rays revealed a dislocated ankle which was badly bruised. She was permitted painkillers and sent home to Ivyleaze to rest. (Over six months later, while in the USA, she discovered that she had chipped a bone.)

Crafty was taking cat naps between our walking sessions. Every time I found him asleep I let him carry on and returned later so as not to disturb him.

In the evening I popped over to Ivyleaze to see how Ginny was. She seemed pleased to see me and showed me a video of the fall. My mouth dropped open as I watched Murphy balloon over the log at the top of the ski jump.

Ginny's ankle had swollen up like a football and she couldn't put any weight on it. It was obviously very painful, but she was putting a brave face on it. I told her not to worry about Crafty as he looked fit and well, which cheered her a little. Crafty was lying in third place. There was no talk of Ginny withdrawing.

I returned to Badminton to clean the tack and prepare for the next day's show jumping, hoping that Ginny would be able to ride. With the Olympics just a few months away, poor Ginny was really under some pressure.

The next morning Heather and Dot arrived early to see Crafty trotted up. Though a little stiff, he looked in good form. It was arranged that I would hack him out for about forty minutes before the official final vetting, and that Louise would trot him up.

When Ginny appeared, wobbling on crutches, she looked pale and drawn.

Uncharacteristically Louise was fussing about a few shavings I had missed on Crafty's day rug. She was worried about trotting up Crafty correctly.

Crafty was duly presented in front of the vets, and passed.

Walking Crafty from the stables to the collecting ring for Sunday's show jumping. Badminton, 1988.

I put him away to relax before the show jumping that afternoon.

At 2 o'clock I rode him up to the collecting ring for the parade of competitors. Ginny, unable to wear her normal riding boot on her swollen leg, had managed to squeeze into a lace-up jodhpur boot. She disguised it with a black bandage from ankle to knee.

What she couldn't disguise was the terrible pain she was in. Once on board, the pain was doubled, but Ginny wasn't in the mood to give in to it.

As I watched Crafty in the arena, I couldn't help feeling that somehow he knew he had to look after his rider. He gave Ginny a clear round and brought her safely back to base. At the end Ginny was dripping with sweat – but relieved. The crowd applauded her courage.

Crafty was placed third, behind Ian Stark's double-act, Sir Wattie and Glenburnie.

As I left the ring after the prize-giving, Crafty swinging along by my side, I couldn't help remembering my first introduction to Badminton, way back in 1984. It was my first attempt at grooming at a three-day event, and I was totally over-awed by it. Now, in 1988, Badminton seemed such a friendly place.

CHAPTER 5

Yard Practice Makes Perfect

The basic routine at the Ivyleaze yard never varies, except for slight seasonal alterations in summer and winter. The rule is to make no sudden changes which could upset the horses in any way.

In the morning someone has to be down on the yard at 6.15 to give the horses a handful of hay or Horsehage to chew on while their feeds are made up. The idea behind this is to stimulate the digestive juices and thereby to ensure efficient breakdown of the forthcoming food.

The feeds are always freshly made up and immediately fed to the horses, allowing a good hour and a half's digestion time before any work is undertaken.

At 6.30 a.m. the other working pupils appear, to begin the day's mucking out etc. The first chore is to put down beds for any horses living out, then to bring in the horses from the fields for their breakfast. During the winter, especially when the weather is poor or when the fields are at their wettest, most of the horses are stabled at night. Occasionally a youngster or a schoolmaster will live out, but Ivyleaze has only eight acres of grazing, so it is important to preserve it as far as possible.

All the horses are bedded on shavings and the beds are mucked out every day. The soiled bedding is carted to a builder's skip by tractor, and when full the skip is removed and replaced by an empty one. To help pack down the shavings we have to jump up and down on them, and sometimes it is difficult to get out of the skip, especially when it is virtually empty.

Water buckets are removed during mucking out; the horses,

meanwhile, are tied up inside their stables for their own safety. The buckets are emptied and refilled (never just topped up), then put back in the stables when the beds are finished.

Once mucking out is completed the horses are brushed off and checked for lumps and bumps. A tail bandage and a mane 'thing' is put on to help lay the mane on the correct side. These 'hoods' are the bane of our lives, and I can't say that the horses are thrilled about them either. We make them ourselves, from the sort of tubular stockinette that is used for polishing cars etc., and cut holes for the horses' eyes and ears. Surprisingly, each one is about ten feet long, but when stretched over the horse's head and neck the length concertinas to a perfect fit. The wither end is secured under the horse's roller.

In theory, the idea is a good one, but in practice we often find that the horses shake their heads violently, flipping their manes over to the wrong side and thus defeating the purpose. In winter, though, the hoods do help to keep the horses'

Sally Kingdon, a working pupil, removing a bag of soaked hay for draining.

necks warm and they can be used to help dry off a horse that has got wet and cold.

We always take the hoods with us whenever we go abroad to compete, much to everyone's amusement. Most people think the horses look silly in them, and laugh. Mind you, they usually approve of the principle.

One person at Ivyleaze is given sole responsibility for weighing, soaking and distributing the daily hay rations. *All* the hay is soaked as a preventive measure – not, as many would assume, because the horses have wind problems or dust allergies. Dry hay contains fungal spores which are taken into the horse's respiratory system as he breathes. Over a period of time the spores gradually build up in the airways and lungs, until ultimately they inhibit the intake of oxygen – which is vital in a competition horse. If hay is soaked for twenty-four hours, the spores swell and fall away into the water.

Individual hay rations are weighed in large porous bags, and each horse has his own bags. When the bags have been drained, they are left outside the horse's stable so that the hay can readily be fed.

Hay is fed in small handfuls throughout the day, especially in winter when it is cold and the horses need something to chew on to keep them warm. Feeding little and often mimmicks the horse's natural grazing method, and prevents a greedy horse from consuming too much before work.

Once the yard chores are finished we pick up the droppings in the fields to help prevent the land becoming horse-sick. The amount of time devoted to this task varies depending on the number of horses that have been turned out. I must admit that it is not a favourite occupation of mine, especially when the fields are wet and muddy.

Breakfasts for the human population are often eaten at great speed. We usually eat in shifts so that the yard is never deserted.

Rotas for the next day's hacking and schooling are worked out each evening by Heather, Dot and Ginny. This means that we can prepare the right horses in the right tack at the right time.

Efforts are made to get the first horses ready for work by 8.30 to 9 a.m., depending on whether they are schooling, jumping, galloping or hacking.

Each groom tacks up the horses for which she is responsible, making sure that they have all four shoes intact and that manes, tails and coats are free from shavings. Brushing boots are always worn in front, sometimes behind, too. Putting them on provides another opportunity to check that the horses' legs are cool and not puffy.

We are always very careful not to put on dirty boots that could chafe, especially around the joints. Woof boots, provided that they are clean, dry and a good fit, have been found to be hard-wearing and cause few rubs.

All the horses go hacking every day (apart from Mondays, which are days off) for one and a half hours. While Heather and the grooms go out for a ride, a couple of novice horses are usually left behind for Ginny to school. When we return from our hack, Ginny schools the advanced horses, who are worked most days unless they are going to the gallops. The horses that Ginny has schooled then go for a hack or to the hills for some fittening work.

Each horse is schooled for thirty to forty-five minutes depending on how well it is going and its stage of training. Obviously the novices are not expected to work in an outline for as long as the advanced horses, but if a horse is being obstinate or learning something new the lesson time could be extended.

Often the manège is quite crowded, with Ginny schooling, Dot lungeing and perhaps someone else riding. To be on the safe side, the rule is always to give way to Ginny, because when she is concentrating she just won't see you – and collisions are not unknown!

After schooling, and weather permitting, the horses are turned out for a spell in the field. In winter, when there isn't much grass about, half an hour is quite long enough for them. If they stay out for longer, they just become bored

Sally, in the yard at Ivyleaze, attending to a horse with an infected toe.

and cold. Generally they are turned out in pairs for company.

In summer they can spend longer in the fields; but the advanced horses, whose diets are closely regulated when they are competing, usually have only an hour a day. Depending on their figures, the other horses stay out from thirty minutes to three hours or more.

In wet weather we turn the horses out in New Zealand rugs with mud-hoods, which also help to keep them warm. If ever I forget to put them on I can guarantee that the horses will come in looking like hippos who have been wallowing in glorious mud.

Novices who are turned out at night are allowed another stint in the field during the day to help prevent boredom setting in.

Strapping is carried out (if possible) straight after a horse has been worked, provided that he isn't too hot. Strapping helps remove scurf and dried sweat, and keeps the coat and skin in good condition. The horse's muscles receive a good massage in the process, so aiding circulation.

Each grooming session is begun by loosening the dirt with a plastic curry comb brushed all over the horse's body, work-

Taking Priceless out to the field. He is wearing boots all round to protect his legs, and is well covered against the elements.

ing in circular movements and with a little more pressure applied over the muscled areas of the neck and rump. Next, the coat is body-brushed, using firmer strokes and more effort, to remove all traces of dirt and debris.

Muddy legs can be tackled with a dandy brush, although thin-skinned, sensitive horses will soon tell you that they prefer a hard body brush instead.

In winter, to help stave off cracked heels, the feathers around the heels and fetlocks are trimmed right back so that the area will dry more quickly. In periods of very wet weather, baby oil is rubbed into the heels to help keep the skin soft and supple.

During the grooming session the feet are picked out and oiled. Careful attention is always paid to the feet, checking for risen clenches, and spread or loose shoes.

The horses are clipped at the beginning of the season: i.e. when they first come in to work in January. The clipping is often done for us over at Badminton by Brian Higham, stud groom to the Duke of Beaufort. At Ivyleaze the stables are too dark and we are short of power points; and anyway, Brian and his helper, Alison Dale, always make such a super job of it.

Lunchtime feeds are given between twelve and one o'clock, by which time we hope to have the yard tidied and swept, and most of the horses exercised and groomed.

During the afternoon we finish any strapping that has to be done, and pull manes and tails as necessary. The horses at Ivyleaze are well turned out at all times, not just at competitions. High standards at home are something in which Heather takes great pride.

Rolling the manège is another task for the afternoons. Firstly, the droppings have to be picked up, then the sides have to be raked level by hand. We take it in turns to drive the small tractor and roller around the arena, avoiding obstacles like jumps and poles. I am ashamed to say that one or two of the surrounding fence posts bear the scars of our activities with the roller.

Each working pupil has her own horses to look after and in addition will be allotted special tasks, like making up the feeds, helping with the cooking or rolling the manège, on a weekly rota basis. Responsibility for hay rations and care of the horse boots are duties which tend to be of a more permanent nature. Routine occasional chores include creosoting fence rails, repainting jumps and poles, even a spot of gardening – all designed to keep the yard and its facilities smart and serviceable.

Tack cleaning is usually left until last as it can easily be done indoors and doesn't require the precious daylight hours. Washing numnahs, boots and bandages are other daily jobs; and we have to keep an eye on the show tack to make sure that it doesn't go mouldy when not in use.

The tack room is quite small and has to be kept tidy, otherwise finding the right rugs and equipment becomes impossible. Everything has to be hung or stored in the right place. In winter, when space is at a premium, it is all too easy to leave a wet New Zealand on top of a dry stable rug unless care is taken.

All the horses wear Lavenham rugs in the stables, over blankets and other rugs if necessary. Thermatex rugs and Witneys are useful, and hollow-filled duvets have proved both warm and light in very cold weather.

Checking the horses for warmth is something of a ritual at Ivyleaze. Whenever anyone goes into a stable they thrust a hand under the rugs at the shoulder and over the loins. Merely feeling the ears can give a false picture, especially if a horse has been looking out of his stable for a while.

The tea-time feeds are given at 5 p.m., by which time we hope to have completed all the main tasks, although we are often behind schedule if we are preparing for a show the next day. Before leaving the yard in the evening we have to doublecheck that the horses are wearing the right rugs, that their water buckets are full, that their kick bolts are done up, and, of course, that they are warm enough.

At 6.30 p.m. someone has to check these things once more, adjusting rugs etc. as necessary, and giving the horses a handful of hay.

Late feeds are given at 9 p.m., at which time water buckets are topped up, the stables are skipped out, tail bandages are removed and the horses are checked for warmth. The bulk of the hay ration is fed now, to give the horses something to chew on through the night.

A typical day's activities would look something like this:

A.M.

6.15   Arrive on yard and give each horse a handful of hay or Horsehage.
         Make up feeds and feed at 6.30.

6.30   Other staff members arrive on yard and begin to muck out.
         Horses who have been out overnight are brought in from the field.
         Whoever is responsible for the hays must drain the pre-soaked hay and remove it from the bath. Once emptied, the bath is refilled and the next batch of weighed-out hays (prepared the day

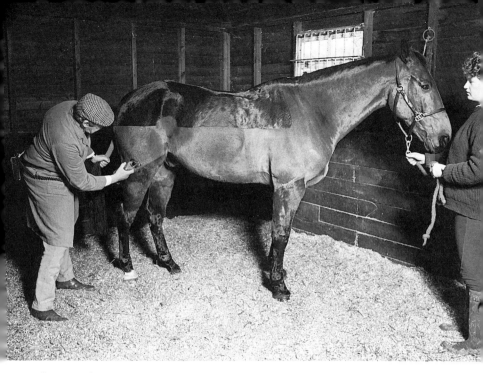

Brian Higham, an expert with the clippers, producing a copy-book blanket clip.

<table>
<tr><td></td><td>before) are put in to soak.</td></tr>
<tr><td></td><td>The horses are mucked out and tidied; mane wraps and tail bandages are put on.</td></tr>
<tr><td></td><td>Fresh water is put in all stables.</td></tr>
<tr><td>7.30</td><td>Someone drives the tractor and muck cart to be emptied in the builder's skip and muck heap.</td></tr>
<tr><td></td><td>Horses are given handfuls of hay while rest of yard staff pick up droppings in the paddocks where horses have been out overnight.</td></tr>
<tr><td></td><td>Sweep yard.</td></tr>
<tr><td>8.00</td><td>Time for breakfast.</td></tr>
<tr><td>8.20</td><td>Horses are tacked up for first hack.</td></tr>
<tr><td>8.30</td><td>First hack leaves yard.</td></tr>
<tr><td></td><td>Ginny begins schooling the first of two horses which we have left behind.</td></tr>
<tr><td>10.15</td><td>First hack arrives back in yard.</td></tr>
</table>

| 10.30-
10.45 | The two horses worked by Ginny go out for a hack of 1-1½ hours, depending on the length of their schooling session. |

| 10.45-
12.00 | Lunchtime feeds are made up and left safely covered or on view in the yard.
Stables are skipped out.
Horses are turned out/brought in from fields.
Grids are set up or dismantled in manège.
Horses who have worked are strapped off.
Handfuls of hay are given out.
Horses are checked for warmth (especially in winter).
Yard tidied and swept. |

P.M.

| 12.00 | Horses who have finished work are fed.
Water buckets are refilled.
Some tack is cleaned (if time permits) and tack room tidied. |

| 1.00 | Lunchtime. |

| 2.00 | Any horses not groomed in the morning are strapped off.
Manes and tails are pulled and trimmed as necessary.
Tack is cleaned.
Handfuls of hay are given out.
Stables are skipped out.
Whoever is responsible for the hays must drain and resoak the night hay for the following day. Hay rations are weighed out for soaking the next morning.
The arena is rolled after Dot has finished teaching.
Horses are brought out for the farrier to shoe.
Coffee is made for the farrier!
Any other relevant jobs are done. |

| 4.30 | Yard is tidied.
Water buckets are checked.
Remaining handfuls of hay are given out. |

Night hay rations are placed outside each horse's
stable.
Stables are skipped out.
Horses are checked for warmth.
Muck cart is emptied again and new shavings are
added to the boxes as necessary.
Feeds are made up for tea.

5.00   Tea-time feeds are given out.
Supper feeds are made up and stored covered in the
feed bins.
Horses are checked for warmth, water, etc.
All stable-door bolts are checked and secured.
Any horses staying out over night are turned out.

6.30   All horses are given a handful of hay.
Horses are checked again for warmth, water, etc.

9.00   Night-time hay is put into stables.
Stables are skipped out and water buckets checked.
Extra rugs are put on if needed.
Horses are given final feeds.
Horses in fields are checked.
Yard is secured for the night.

The feeding regime at Ivyleaze follows the golden rules that
apply to all equines: e.g. the horses are fed little and often,
and according to work, age, temperament, etc. Feeds buckets
are never used for any other purpose, and are scrubbed clean
every time they are used. Feed mangers are also washed out
daily whenever possible.

When the horses are in hard work they receive four feeds a
day, with at least four hours in between each feed. The basic
feed, known in the yard as 'slops', consists of:

1 scoop of soaked chaff
½ scoop of sugar-beet
½ scoop of grass meal

The sugar-beet and grass meal come in nut form and

are soaked for twenty-four hours before feeding. Horses receiving four meals per day have their intake of sugar-beet and grass meal reduced to a quarter or a third depending on their waistline.

The hard feed is milled by Spillers, and in the main we use their Special Event Cubes and bruised oats. Novice horses are also allowed a coarse mix. The latter is not suitable for the horses competing under FEI rules as Spillers cannot guarantee that it is free from minute traces of forbidden (though naturally occurring) substances. This means that if a horse is taking part in an official three-day event it has to be weaned off the coarse mix at least two weeks before the competition, otherwise there is a risk of failing a dope test.

Heather and Dot work out the amounts of hard feed each horse is to receive. Often they refer back to feeding records from a previous year for guidance.

Horses who are injured, sick or off work are fed slops only. This helps reduce the possibility of a protein build-up in the system and thereby avoids problems such as filled legs and azoturia.

On rest days one or two meals are replaced by slops, depending on the individual and whether he has a tendency to be fresh.

During the winter months the horses are also fed boiled or micronised barley. The boiled barley isn't suitable once the horses start to do fast work, but it helps to keep weight on the novices. The barley grains are soaked for twenty-four hours to help soften the outer husk and to lessen the cooking time. An old Burco boiler simmers the barley efficiently, even if it does fill the tack room with steam and make everything damp.

The chaff is freshly cut once a week using an old chaff cutter converted to electricity. When I first arrived at Ivyleaze we had to use a manual chaff cutter, which was heavy going but excellent for building up fitness. The chaff consists of two-thirds oat straw to one third hay, and like the hay it has to be soaked before feeding. It adds bulk to the feed and prevents the horses from bolting their meals. (Bran is never

'Where's my lunch?' Priceless, wearing his mane hood, cranes his neck to watch the preparations in the feed room.

fed because it contains phytin, a substance which deprives the blood of calcium, and it is of no real nutritional value.)

Heather buys all her hay and oat straw from a local farmer. She always chooses very good quality seed hay, and care is taken never to waste any because it is so expensive.

Ever since Priceless contracted leptospirosis, Heather has been very diligent about keeping the yard vermin-free. All forage is stored off the ground, and all feedstuffs are kept in tightly lidded feed bins (that is, when I remember to shut them!). Regular visits from a well-known firm of pest controllers ensures that the numbers are kept down. Once, though, the rat man came face to face with a live rat and I swear I have never seen anyone run backwards so fast.

Most of the horses at Ivyleaze are good doers and we don't have much trouble with fussy feeders. Occasionally horses receiving slops leave their chaff, but once hard food is introduced they usually hoover everything up and lick the

73

Jack, caught in the act of demolishing one of the hanging baskets which Heather puts up to decorate the yard in summer.

mangers till they shine. If any horse doesn't eat up all its hay, the ration is cut down and a few pounds of Horsehage substituted to help restore the bulk element of the diet. Because Horsehage is so rich we never feed more than half the weight of the hay ration.

The stables are all 12ft × 12ft, apart from the two bigger boxes where the big boys live. A few years ago eye-level hay racks were removed and new ones fitted at about chest height so that the horses' heads and necks have to stretch down, not up, to eat their hay. Hay racks fitted at head height help develop underneck muscles, which is not desirable. They can also cause hay and seeds to fall into the horses' eyes, ears and nostrils. The feed mangers are fixed in an opposite corner.

Every working pupil has two or three boxes to muck out or beds to make up. Day beds are always put up at night so that the floor has a chance to air and dry.

All the horses are treated as individuals, and indeed no two horses are the same. Horses with bad stable habits are avoided at all costs, and during my stay we have never had any problems. Sometimes new horses can be difficult to handle, but with patience and care they soon change their ways.

On the whole, the horses are very sound. Every effort is made to ensure that their fitness is built up slowly and that strain to tendons and muscles is avoided. Occasionally a horse will twist a pastern or fetlock, but that doesn't mean a long lay off.

Someone was once heard to say that Ginny was very lucky with her horses. Luck may indeed play a small part – but it is the Ivyleaze system, with its attention to detail and its sound training methods, that gives Ginny's horses a head start in competitions. Couple that with Ginny's exceptional ability as a rider and it's not difficult to see why the Ivyleaze team so often picks up the ribbons.

'Hay, look at me!' And to think that part of the reason we lowered the hay racks was to prevent hay falling into the horses' eyes.

CHAPTER 6

Training

At Ivyleaze there is a tried and tested system for building
up the horses' fitness. The method is based on years of
experience and there is no doubt that it works.

In January, the horses come back in to work after their
winter holidays, to prepare for the forthcoming eventing
season. Before they begin, their manes and tails are pulled,
their coats are clipped, their feathers are trimmed, and their
feet are shod. To reacquaint them with the feel of wearing a
bridle and saddle, Dot lunges them quietly in the school.

Once shod they are gently hacked out daily for an hour or
so, gradually increasing to one and a half hours over the next
three weeks. During this time they also go into the school for
revision lessons in flatwork, or to be lunged. This early work
in the manège is mainly carried out in walk, with short periods
of trotting, each session lasting about twenty to thirty minutes. The schooling time is deducted from the overall exercise
time, not added to it.

Ginny likes to work the horses in the school on most days,
but each horse's performance and attitude is carefully monitored and his work plan adjusted to suit him.

As a rule, Mondays are rest days for the horses. Instead of
being put to work they are given a thorough strapping, and
turned out for a while to relax.

By the middle of week five, the horses have done enough
road work, plus trotting and cantering in the school, to enable
them to be taken for bursts of more sustained cantering. At
this stage they might tackle a total of eight or ten minutes

of cantering, split into two halves and with an intervening period of relaxation at the walk.

At the end of the week grid work over a series of low jumps might be introduced. By now the total work time for each horse is about two hours.

The land around Ivyleaze is fairly flat, so whenever we want to do some hill work we have to box the horses and drive to Castle Coombe. There the hacking is very hilly, and the horses enjoy the change of scene.

Over the next four weeks the length of the cantering sessions is built up, until by week ten the horses can manage a total of fifteen minutes' cantering, which helps build up their stamina. A short pipe-opening gallop is also introduced about this time.

The horses are given two canter sessions per week, usually on Wednesdays and at the weekend.

The fast work is mostly carried out at Jeremy Tree's gallops at Calne. The gallops, made of shavings, are about six furlongs in length and laid out with a right-handed bend and an upward slope near the end, which helps in the fittening work.

Meanwhile the jumping and grid work is building up all the time, and the flatwork – to increase suppleness and flexibility – is becoming more demanding.

Throughout the fitness programme each horse is watched closely, and Ginny, Dot and Heather decide if a particular horse needs, say, sharpening up with more speed work, or whether his stamina work should be increased. Feeding in relation to work is another matter which comes under close scrutiny. The emphasis is on building up the horses *slowly*, no matter if a competition is looming.

All being well, by week twelve the horses are ready to tackle their first event of the season. To help to prepare them for the atmosphere of a competition they are usually taken to a show jumping competition or two beforehand.

Ginny likes to carry out all the fast work herself. Whenever she goes cantering, one of the grooms goes with her, riding the second horse. I consider myself fortunate in that I have been allowed to canter all Ginny's horses, even Priceless whom she normally reserved strictly for herself. The advanced horses motor along like Roll-Royces, with effortless strides and in beautiful balance. They teach you what to look for when trying to school the novices.

The general exercise rotas are worked out by Heather, who carries out a lot of the hacking herself. Her hacks are often quite interesting, especially when we are riding in foreign territory. I remember hacking in the woods at an event at Tweseldown and being told to keep a close eye out for passing tanks!

The horses are hacked out in company, never alone. This helps them to relax and enjoy their daily outings. Heather insists that the horses have to be kept walking forward on a long rein, but with a contact. This means that you have to concentrate all the time, until the habit becomes ingrained. Once the technique has been mastered you can snatch a few moments for a gossip – but making sure that you don't neglect your duty, as Heather is quick to spot any shortcomings. Every so often the horses are allowed a free rein to stretch and relax their neck muscles. This is especially important for the youngsters who aren't used to working and haven't built up the right muscles.

The roads around Ivyleaze are often quite busy, which poses problems if your horse is traffic-shy. Noddy, particularly, liked to play on the fact that he was wary of heavy lorries. Nine times out of ten you could guarantee an encounter with a huge farm vehicle or coach whenever you went out on him. In one incident we executed a very neat pirouette by the side of the road and popped over a wall into the adjoining cornfield. This presented another problem, as the only way out was the way we had come!

One of the worst moments I had out hacking involved my fellow groom Nicks. She was riding Ben along the road in front of me: just as a lorry was passing us, Ben, with no sense of timing, spooked at something in the hedge. The lorry didn't slow down and I watched helplessly as one of Ben's hind legs disappeared underneath it. Miraculously no

Dot lungeing in the manège. Her lungeing technique can always be relied upon to improve a horse's way of going.

Dot, dressed for the Arctic, preparing to lunge Murphy in the snow-covered manège. No matter what the weather, work goes on.

harm was done – but the lorry had ripped the strap off Ben's boot. Some horses, like cats, have nine lives.

Another series of incidents occurred when hacking to Badminton Park, on what started out as a fairly routine sort of day.

One morning it was arranged that I would ride one novice and lead another to the Park at Badminton. There I was to meet up with Ginny, who had been given permission to jump a couple of logs and rails of the training fences.

Just as I arrived at the Park gates, the horse I was leading suddenly pricked up his ears and stiffened his neck. Next, he jammed on the brakes and wheeled round, practically pulling me out of the saddle. Realising that his freedom had not yet been granted, he put in an almighty buck and yanked the reins out of my hand. I watched in horror as he scampered off down the road, heading towards another entrance gate. Gathering my wits I trotted off after him, not daring to canter lest I scare him further. Eventually, and much to my relief, I found him loitering in the stable courtyard at Badminton House, unsure what to do next.

Thankful that he had come to no harm, I set off for the meeting point without further mishap.

After Ginny had schooled both the horses, I was instructed to take them straight home. I decided to ride the miscreant to avoid a repeat of the earlier performance, and to lead the other, more steady individual.

I hadn't been on board two seconds when, quite without warning, the horse went into reverse gear. He started running backwards and spinning round, anything but go forwards. Eventually I calmed him down and Ginny decided to ride him out of the Park herself to show him who was boss. By the time we had reached the village, just outside the Park, the horse was still very tense, so Ginny continued to ride him for a little longer until he relaxed. After that I led him home.

At lunchtime I received a message that I was to take that same horse back to the Park and meet Ginny at 2.30 p.m. What I didn't know was that I had been given only half the message...

A wintry view of Badminton House, taken on a quiet November day. Hacking through the beautiful Park at Badminton is one of the most enjoyable aspects of work at Ivyleaze.

I set off in good time and arrived at the Park gates at the appointed hour. On the way there I passed Lord Patrick Beresford on the road and he asked me if Ginny was at Ivyleaze. I told her that she would probably be setting off on her way to meet me.

The horse seemed relaxed and I walked him around, just inside the entrance while we were waiting. After a while we ambled down the road for a change of scene. As we turned to come back, I felt his whole body stiffen. He stopped dead in his tracks, as though he had turned to stone. For a minute or two nothing I did had any effect whatsoever. I used my legs and encouraged him by patting him and soothing him with my voice. Suddenly, he lurched into action, backing on to a grass verge and edging his way towards a fence. Realising that he could go no further, he reared. I urged him to go forward, but he wouldn't have it. Up he went again, this time coming down on his left shoulder, trapping my leg with his weight.

He struggled to his feet, and I found that I still had hold of the reins. Picking myself up, I flexed my leg to see if there

81

was any sign of life in it. At that moment the horse pulled back and reared again. As he did so he went straight over backwards and came crashing down on the ground. I thought myself fortunate that I wasn't underneath him.

Free at last, he fled into Badminton Park – and disappeared into the heavy mist that was falling.

'Brilliant,' I thought. 'You've really done it now, Elaine.'

I limped towards the gates. Then, hearing the sound of horses behind me, I turned back. Some riders were on their way home, their day's hunting having been cancelled because of poor visibility. I explained what had happened, and one of them was kind enough to lend me a horse.

I rode off into the Park, confronted by an impossible task. Of course, he was nowhere to be seen, and I returned to the Park gates feeling very anxious indeed about the whole affair. I remembered how it had all started. I was meant to meet Ginny. If only she had been there!

Another thoughtful person offered to drive me round the Park – and we eventually found the horse sulking in a corner.

I brought him back round to the road, to be met by three very concerned people – Ginny, Heather and Dorothy – wanting to know the answers to a few questions.

Without waiting for a full explanation, Ginny was about to get on board, when we were treated to an action replay of his earlier behaviour. As he backed away, Heather went to reprimand him. And again he flew off down the road and into the Park.

Tempers were now frayed all round. I thought I'd better find him – and quickly.

He was lurking in the same place where I had found him before. We caught him quite easily, and Ginny was legged up into the saddle. The pair set off towards the Park gates, arguing all the way.

In another of his temper tantrums he actually managed to unseat her with his plunging. She jumped straight back into the saddle, and when he had calmed down a little she made arrangements for him to stay the night at the Badminton stables, where he could reflect on his actions.

That night after supper the story of the day's happenings was pieced together. It seems that Ginny had been waiting for me in the village while I was waiting for her at the Park gate. As the vital snip of information about our meeting-place hadn't been given to me, I had assumed that we would rendezvous at the Park entrance, as we had done in the morning. There had been a slight hiccup in communications. Luckily no one was hurt (except my leg, which had been a little squashed).

The horse in question did improve over a period of time and was eventually able to walk through his 'black spot' near the Park without tensing up. We never did discover what caused his sudden and irrational behaviour at that particular place.

Schooling in the manège was usually carried out under Dot's watchful eye. Ginny always schooled the advanced horses. The length of time devoted to schooling and the movements performed depend on the ability of the horse and on its stage of training. The rider's ability and her stage of training are also taken into consideration, and we are helped and corrected by Dot as we go along. Sometimes horses and riders learn together in Dot's lessons.

I have had to commit to memory and put into practice three basic rules:

CONTROLLED FORWARD IMPULSION
EVEN RHYTHM IN ALL PACES
CORRECT BEND IN ALL MOVEMENTS

These three simple tenets form the foundation of every horse's training at Ivyleaze.

To help with the finer points of dressage riding, Ginny has always relied on Pat Manning, and during the run-up to a major competition Ginny books a series of lessons. Often, Pat comes over to the yard for a morning to watch Ginny and the horses work.

As part of the suppling routine, Dot works the horses on the lunge. She believes that lungeing tack should be kept simple, and has never resorted to the use of gadgets: though she does use plain leather side reins, preferring them to the type with elasticated inserts which can encourage horses to lean.

Our lungeing cavesson is a little unusual, in that it has a drop noseband and is very lightweight. It gives excellent control over the horses' actions.

The horses are lunged with and without riders, to help them with their balance. A rider can influence and regulate the horse's rhythm as well as being able to develop a deeper seat. For a change the rider can concentrate on herself instead of worrying about the horse's way of going.

We are sometimes asked to lay out trotting poles, which encourage the horses to come off their forehand and to lengthen or shorten the trot strides. Jumps, too, are erected for the novices to tackle without a rider, which helps to freshen them up.

Care is taken to work the horses evenly on both reins. If a horse is a little stiff on one side, then extra attention is paid to suppling that side of him, but never at the expense of the good side.

Work goes on in the arena whatever the heavens throw at us. Dot certainly won't give in to a little thing called weather. However, there are occasions when the wintry cold gets the better of her (it is much colder standing on the ground teaching than it is riding on a lesson). SOS messages then go out for steaming mugs of Bovril or coffee to thaw her out.

Ginny's dog, Oxo – a pint-sized, Irish black and tan terrier – is absolutely devoted to his mistress and loves to come out into the arena whenever she's schooling. His favourite game is to dash here and there behind Ginny's horse, which can be quite distracting. Sometimes the Rottweiler, Elsa, will join in the fun, and I once saw her going over the trotting poles behind a horse that Dot was lungeing – that is, until she realised that it was hard work and not as exciting as it first looked.

Once fit, the horses are jumped at least once a week: the novices possibly more often. Series of grids are favoured, to improve the horses' athleticism and to make them quicker on their feet. Ginny usually gives us details of the grids that she plans to use next day, and the working pupils set up the wings etc. in advance. We are allowed to watch the horses jumping in between moving poles or rebuilding fences. Learning how Ginny and Dot resolve a particular jumping problem has proved a useful education.

Generally the fences we put up are never any higher than those the horses will meet at an event.

Cross-country schooling is fitted in when time and the weather permit. We travel the horses to Wylye, which is an excellent training ground as there is such a variety of well-constructed fences with different aspects and levels of difficulty. Although Lord and Lady Hugh Russell, who owned the course and built the jumps, have moved away the fences can still be used for schooling.

Lady Hugh is a brilliant fence designer. Because her ingenious fences at Wylye made the best possible use of the lie of the land, they are a pleasure to jump, and the horses clearly enjoy them, too. Lady Hugh is also a most talented trainer and can tell a rider exactly how to approach and ride any fence. She can spot faults almost before they develop, and

Elsa, the Rottweiler, chasing Jack to make sure he trots on!

knows precisely how to correct them.

She used to conduct lessons from behind the wheel of a Mini-Moke, which she drove at a rate of knots, keeping up with the horses as they progressed from fence to fence. Passengers could absorb the wisdom of her remarks from the back of her Moke, and it was not unknown for people to fall out as the little jeep bumped its way around the course.

Nearer home is a course at Sherston, owned by Derek Sidebottom. He has a range of friendly fences that are suitable for novices, especially those on their first time out. Unfortunately there aren't many other places to go to, which at times proves a problem.

Dot and Heather always come along to watch the cross-country schooling. They take such a keen interest in each horse's progress that it is only natural they want to see how he fares over the log piles, ditches and drops, etc. They make a note of anything they see which they feel could be useful for future competitions.

The tack used on the horses is basically straightforward – no schooling devices or gadgets of any kind are employed to cut corners. Many of the horses go well on the flat in plain rubber snaffles. The choice of bit depends on the horse's way of going. A French link or loose-ring snaffle might be tried if a horse is leaning or heavy. Sometimes we will try a whole range of bits to find the one that best suits a particular horse.

Each horse has a set of everyday tack that is kept in good repair by Judy Groves, a local woman who is skilled at altering and repairing leatherwork. The horses' 'Sunday best' bridles are kept solely for use at shows.

Some of the yard's nicest leatherwork was bought by Heather several years ago from a saddler based in Devon. More latterly, Ginny has linked up with the Walsall saddlery firm, Barnsby, who now supply her. The latest Barnsby Leng bridles are two-tone brown and look extremely smart. They are kept for dressage only.

The nosebands on the bridles are mostly of the cavesson

Putting up a jump for Ginny in the manège. We never practise over fences higher than those the horse will meet in competition.

type. If a horse persistently opens his mouth or crosses his jaw flash and grakle nosebands are fitted. Flash nosebands are used mainly for flatwork, although sometimes Ginny opts for a grakle. She did this once to her cost when riding Murphy in a dressage competition. We had forgotten that grakles were not permitted, and she was eliminated.

Martingales are worn only if needed. The fitting depends on the individual.

Ginny's favourite dressage saddle is an old Kieffer to which she had become rather attached. In the past she rode in a Stübben Parsival, until she discovered the Kieffer and swapped her allegiance.

The jumping saddles are usually Stübben Siegfrieds, though sometimes a novice will wear something different. Lately Ginny has been involved in the design of a jumping saddle built with cross-country riding in mind. She wanted a saddle that was forward-cut enough to be comfortable, and with a flatter seat to allow the rider's weight to shift backwards, particularly at drop fences. She also stipulated that it should give the rider the feeling that his or her leg is close to the horse's side and not pushed away from it at all.

After several attempts and much discussion, I believe Barnsbys have come up with a saddle that answers Ginny's requirements. As I write, it is being broken in for use at competitions.

After a three-day event the horses who have taken part are given a complete break from work. They are walked out for about a week, to let them unwind and relax. Their feeds are reduced and their hay or grazing time increased to compensate. Once on holiday they usually have their shoes removed so that if they play around in the field they won't come to much harm.

The holiday period lasts from four to six weeks during the season, longer if it coincides with the winter. A lot depends on when the horse is next due to compete.

The novices are also given a spell off work during the season. This helps to take the pressure off them and gives them time to relax. Ginny never likes pushing youngsters too hard. The aim is to produce a horse that is a willing partner, right from the start. Too many talented youngsters are spoilt by ambitious riders forging ahead too quickly – but not at Ivyleaze.

CHAPTER 7

Slow Progress

One of the main reasons for working at Ivyleaze was that I wanted the chance to improve my riding. At home I had always done quite well at local shows, and I thought myself an average-to-good rider. Cross-country riding was my love, right from the start. Dressage was something that had to be put up with if you wanted to event; show jumping could be tolerable, even fun, on the right horse, and with practice. More than anything, I wanted to event.

However, when I arrived at Ivyleaze it quickly became apparent that everything I had learned over the last sixteen years would have to be thrown right out of the window if I wanted to make any progress at all. I fell to earth more with a thud than a bump.

Those early days at Ivyleaze were not easy for me. I was struggling along, trying desperately to keep my head above water. There was so much to learn and I was alarmed to find that I kept forgetting things, which was something I had never done at home. Home felt like a million miles away. People would ask me if I was home-sick and I'd say, 'Not really.' Funny, everyone else could see it, but not me.

As far as my riding was concerned, the first thing that had to change was my position. Looking at old photographs I can see now that my lower legs were at least six inches too far forward, and I can remember that my hands were very set. Heather often says that she wishes she had a video of my early riding style, a thought which makes me cringe.

Slowly, things did improve but it's hard not to revert to old habits, especially when a tricky situation arises.

In the first year, I rode Titch a lot – and what a long-

Diddy, my 14.2 hh mare, and I proudly displaying the Haydon Hunt trophy, presented for winning the junior section of the 1981 Hunt Race across country.

suffering, patient horse he was to put up with me. I was actually allowed to take him to Badgeworth to do a dressage test. Not surprisingly I found it difficult to keep all 17.2 hh of him together and on the bridle. I failed miserably. How I tried to get him on the bit, but it was no use. I used every ounce of strength I had to pull him into an outline, but, of course, I wasn't using enough leg and Titch was more than a match for my arms. In his own way he was teaching me a lesson, but I was too blind to see it at the time.

This outing put a stop to my competitive efforts for a while and I went back to the drawing board. I worked hard in the school and whenever I hacked out I tried to improve and strengthen my leg position.

Shortly after this, Heather decided that my feel should be improved and that I should learn to follow the movement of the horse's head without dropping the contact. I had to make sure that the reins never went slack as I rode. Later I learned to do this by just relaxing my arms, especially the shoulders, and allowing the horse to do the work for me. I had to learn to *carry* my arms, though, so that my hands didn't drop on to the withers.

My best teacher for this technique was a horse called Spotless, an Irish gelding that Ginny had bought. I must have hacked out on Spotless solidly for about three months, which seemed like a lifetime. At the end of this period I was allowed to school him under Ginny's watchful eye and she gave me tips on how to improve him.

By now my leg position was more as it should be, with my thighs further back underneath me. Gradually, shoulder, hip and heel were coming into line. My aim was to learn to use my legs in this position, as they were nowhere near strong enough to back up my hand; and I had to eliminate my tendency to use the hand before the leg.

I started to school Titch again. Meanwhile, Mark Todd was competing on both Spotless and Titch. It was good to see them going so well for him – which was more attributable to the fact that Mark is such a great horseman with tremendous feel than to the fact that I had helped to school them.

My basic problems on the flat were reflected in my jumping. Until my position improved I wasn't allowed to jump at all.

Slowly I was learning to think of more than one thing at a time. For example, I was to lighten my seat in downward transitions whilst allowing with my hands, so that the horse could go forward into the chosen pace. This way he wouldn't be restricted in front and throw up his head.

Just three months after I arrived at Ivyleaze I found myself grooming for Ginny and Night Cap at my first Badminton. I was totally overwhelmed, and the event remains a blur in my mind. Friends tell me that I wore a bewildered expression on my face the whole time, and whenever the subject of that particular Badminton is mentioned, Dot and Heather just raise their eyebrows.

The things that stick in my mind most are all the mistakes I made. After giving Night Cap his last feed before the cross-country I forgot to turn off the automatic drinker in his stable. I was walking up to the trade stands with another groom when I suddenly realised what I had done. I ran full tilt back to the stables to find that Heather and Dot had discovered my error and turned the water off themselves. Thereafter I was literally spoon-fed with instructions from Dot, and I think I must have carried them out like a zombie.

Another thing that I remember from Badminton '84 is that someone walked off with Ginny's cross-country stick as a memento, which made me very angry. In fact, it wasn't a good Badminton all round, as Ginny suffered a fall from Night Cap at the lake fence.

In the autumn of '84 I started doing some grid work with Ben, one of the youngsters who we were bringing on. He was fun to ride and very quick with his feet and his brain.

To begin with I had a tendency to be in front of the movement when jumping, so I was taught to wait and go with the horse, using my hips more to bring my weight back.

It was about this time that Heather talked to me about my future. I had been at Ivyleaze for about ten months and had at last learned to trust the system and not to fight against it. In her usual direct manner Heather told me that she thought I had only made headway in the last month or so, and that I didn't have what it took to be a competitor. Frankly, I was shocked. All my life I had competed, and as far as I was concerned I had made a pretty good job of it. I decided to stay on – if only to prove that my attitude wasn't so wrong, and that if I put my mind to it I could show them what I was capable of. I felt that I had given up a lot to come to Ivyleaze, and since I had chosen this particular path I wanted to see it through. I did not want to accept failure.

From then on I started to try to ask a lot more questions about my riding in an effort to understand what I had to do to improve. Being a bit of a loner I found it difficult to talk to Heather, Dot and Ginny and I think I retreated into my shell more than I should have done.

As luck would have it, a new working pupil, Wendy Tyrrell, joined the ranks and she and I became good friends.

Wendy was very supportive and eased the communication problems. I still tried to keep a low profile and went out of my way to avoid getting into trouble.

Nothing escaped Heather's watchful eye and she noticed that I had been working extra hard to improve. As a reward I was allowed to enter both Ben and Bally, another youngster, in a dressage-with-jumping competition at Larkhill.

Oh dear, what a fiasco!

I'm afraid I became a little confused in the dressage tests, losing my way when my mind went blank. To make matters worse, in the show jumping Ben decided to show me who was boss. We cleared the first few fences without a hitch, then he started to spook, and I dropped my whip. Being quick on the uptake, he exploited the situation to the full – and then he really had some fun with me. After more stops and starts than I care to remember, we were eliminated. As I left the arena it was not necessary for anyone to speak – their faces said it all.

I had no time to stop and wallow in it; I had Bally to ride

Riding Priceless at Badminton in 1985.

immediately afterwards. He was a real friend and restored a little of my shattered confidence with a lovely clear round.

Ginny took Ben in hand and managed to enter him hors concours in the next class. He attempted to spook with her, too, but being so much stronger in her legs, she guided him round after a smack or two, which gained his attention.

They say that horses are great levellers. Just when I thought I was beginning to get somewhere, dear Ben showed me how far I had to go.

After our illustrious performance it was decided that I would ride Bally in future and Ginny would ride Ben to bring him into line. At least I wasn't relegated out of competitions altogether.

In 1985 Priceless and Night Cap were entered for Badminton and I had to groom for them both. I was helped by Nicks, who joined me when her work at Ivyleaze was done. I had never groomed for Priceless at a three-day event before, but I knew that he could be a rascal. He became even more ticklish to groom, especially if anyone was looking. I had to keep a protective eye out for any unwitting spectators who passed our stables as he didn't like being 'poked about' while looking over the door.

Both the horses performed well in the dressage. Night Cap managed to relax and picked up some good marks, while Priceless became indignant when Ginny asked for a canter up the centre line and gave her a buck instead. Priceless, being Priceless, did at least manage to come down on the right lead.

Although the going on the cross-country was wet, it certainly didn't bother my two warriors. Night Cap, who went early, was clear with just a few time faults. He must have told Priceless how easy it was, because Priceless was raring to go and couldn't wait to get out on the course. He produced a brilliant clear and stepped into third place behind Mark Todd on Charisma and Torrance Fleischmann-Watkins on Finvarra. Clever old Night Cap was lying fourth.

Sunday's show jumping proved to be something of a nail-biting affair. Night Cap and Priceless took the fences in their stride and went clear. I was too busy with the horses to watch Charisma and Finvarra go round, but gasps from the crowd told us that fences were falling.

Amid much confusion and disbelief we discovered that Priceless had won. Night Cap had finished in third place.

Ginny's sponsor, Roger Davies, managing director of British National Life, was overjoyed and proud that he would be going into the arena to receive Night Cap's rosette from the Queen. Suddenly he remembered his footwear – he had to wear wellies in his moment of glory!

That night at Ivyleaze, while everyone was reliving the cross-country on video, I fell fast asleep in front of the telly.

After the excitement of Badminton, life at Ivyleaze returned to normal. After a few cross-country practices I was preparing for my first ever Novice BHS one-day event, at Wokingham. It was decided that I should ride Bally while Ginny rode Crafty and Ben.

I walked the course with Dot and Ginny and felt it was a fair one for novices.

For once I didn't make a hash of the dressage: at least, I didn't go wrong; and our show jumping was clear, thanks to Bally's generosity. As the moment arrived for our cross-country onslaught, we set off with gusto. Everything was going smoothly until we reached the water jump. Bally dug his toes in and said he wasn't getting wet for love nor money. I'd done it again. We were eliminated.

I walked slowly back to the lorry, passing Dot and Heather on the way. As I drew closer I could see smoke.

'Why didn't you jump the alternative?' they asked.

I looked blankly at their faces.

'What alternative?'

I hadn't walked the easier route, being totally unaware that there was one. This made me feel even worse about the whole thing.

We stayed at the competition until all the riders had completed their cross-country rounds so that we could practise going through the water (the organisers had kindly given

Bally and I, all togged up for our first BHS event at Wokingham in 1985.

us permission). Heather brought along a lunge whip, just in case. After a brief argument, Bally thought that perhaps he would jump it after all, so I popped him over a couple of times to gain his confidence. We moved to another water splash fence, at which he hesitated, but after a sharp reminder from yours truly he went through that one as well.

Heather didn't seem too dismayed about our performance, but I'm afraid I felt awful about it. I always had the feeling that people had odd ideas about an Ivyleaze horse who was being ridden by someone other than Ginny. After all, if the horse was any good, Ginny would be riding it herself. In reality this wasn't the case – often Ginny simply had too many to ride. Looking back, I think I spent far too much time imagining what other people thought instead of getting on with the job in hand.

I took part in a few more competitions and managed not to disgrace myself. My dressage was proving to be my weak link and I was having trouble getting Bally on the bit: that is, until Ginny sorted me out. Quite how she did it we don't know, but from then on I never looked back. The next day we clocked up our first points by coming fifth at Bourton. I can't tell you how good it felt to collect that rosette.

I was asked to groom for Priceless at the European Championships at Burghley in 1985. This was the first team event I had been involved in and I learned a lot from the experience. A couple of the other grooms were old hands at the game and kindly showed me the ropes. Before the competition itself the team members and their grooms had to attend a team 'concentration' at Wylye, Lord and Lady Hugh's superb training centre in Wiltshire.

On the day, the team went really well (save poor Tiny Clapham who had a nasty fall) and Ginny won the individual gold medal. We were having a fantastic year, winning Badminton and the European Championships in the space of a few months.

At competitions I'm always so caught up with the horses and their needs that I never take in what is happening around me. It wasn't until I saw the video afterwards that the message sunk in. Watching it, I allowed myself to feel proud that I had had a hand in turning out that fit, gleaming horse so bravely tackling his fences.

During the winter of '85 Bally was sold on and I started to ride Freeway ('Noddy' to us). He was a big 16.2 hh. Thoroughbred type of horse who hadn't done any competing. He was a very loose-limbed horse who moved well, but I couldn't produce the best from him on the flat. Then, one day, Ginny gave me a talking to about not being afraid to use the bit to help me, and thenceforth we started to click. It seems that when you've been told for so long that you have bad hands, you daren't use them for fear of doing the wrong thing.

By now my contact had improved and my hands were not so harsh and set. Also, I was able to use them independently and back them up with the leg. I was beginning to function as a rider – just beginning.

Early in 1986 Ginny was away for quite a spell on holiday, which gave me the opportunity to do more schooling and to jump the horses through grids. Dot and I worked hard, particularly with Crafty, putting him through different combinations so that he learned to adjust his stride and to fold up his legs. At one stage we went down a grid of six bounces (gradually built up, of course). I also rode him on the lunge over poles and on 10-metre circles in canter so that he learned not only to balance himself but also to maintain that balance with the weight of a rider.

Ben and Noddy, too, were put through their paces. Each of the horses was very different, a factor which helped my riding as I had to adapt my style to theirs.

1986 was not one of my better years, but it was a good one for Ginny and Priceless. When preparing to go to the World Championships in Gawler, Australia, I made a silly mistake over the feed. When it was discovered by Heather, she gave me a rocket. If my visa, etc., hadn't been organised I think she would gladly have sent someone else. During the flight I sulked about my stupidity and decided to try harder.

Priceless was in terrific form in Australia and claimed the gold medal for his efforts. Throughout the competition I tried to keep my head down, but irritatingly I made another stupid blunder by oversleeping one morning. This fact, like most of my mistakes, did not go unnoticed and Heather and Dot had to send Bill, the farrier, to wake me.

On returning to England I gritted my teeth and got on with my job.

Noddy and I were progressing quite well on the flat and in our cross-country, but we had a slight difference of opinion about our show jumping. Being a big horse he was difficult to keep together and often he was more in charge than his rider. The crunch came at a competition at Brendon Hills where we managed to clock up 50 jumping penalties, in a manner which I'd rather not describe.

Dot and Heather decided that something had to be done. Rider Mandy Hosp was to take over Noddy and sort him out. Ginny, knowing how I felt about the matter, tried to make light of it, but my spirits were too low to take notice.

I threw myself into my work and tried to forget about my own failings. Crafty went to France for his first three-day event and I was invited to groom Yair for Ian Stark, who was also making the trip.

Ian was very different to work for – so laid back and

relaxed. I am sure he thought it strange that I should be asking him for the times when he would be riding. I think he normally arrived when he was ready.

Crafty went well and finished fourth. Ginny was pleased, but still not convinced about him. Heather was absolutely delighted.

That autumn Murphy went to Burghley and surprised everyone by winning it. He was taken there more for the experience than for the competition. By the end of the cross-country he was still pulling very hard, and so began the search for a bit that could match his strength.

By winning Burghley, Murphy showed the eventing world that it was the Ivyleaze system that produced winners, not just the horse's breeding.

About this time I started to ride a horse called Stevie who was with us for a while. Stevie had a short, choppy stride when he first arrived but once we slowed him down we found he could move quite well. He was by a horse called Hill Farmer, and true to his line this little horse could jump. Stevie taught me a valuable lesson: not to hang on when a horse pulls against you.

At the beginning of 1987 I was introduced to a young

Going out for a hack on Taffy, a four-year-old chestnut gelding, in the winter of 1986.

chestnut horse called Taffy, out of an Argentinian polo pony by River Poaching. We got along quite well and he was a genuine soul who tolerated my show-jumping technique, which was going through a bad patch at the time. For some inexplicable reason I had lost the ability to see a stride before a jump. To help me, Dot put up a fence in the manège and asked me to jump it. I must have jumped it at least half a dozen times and each time we took off at a different place.

To begin with Taffy was very much on his forehand, which didn't make my job any easier.

One day Ginny, who was watching my pathetic efforts, reminded me that the priority was to get over the fence. The penny dropped. I had been so busy worrying about balancing the horse, about making sure that he was straight, about going forward out of the corner, etc., that I had lost sight of the fundamental aim.

That night Ginny gave me a poem to read:

> If you think you are beaten, you are.
> If you think you dare not, you don't.
> If you'd like to win but think you can't
> It's almost certain that you won't.
> If you think you'll lose, you've lost.
> For out of the world we find
> Success begins with a fellow's will –
> It's all in the state of mind.
> If you think you're out classed, you are.
> You've got to think high to rise.
> You've got to be sure of yourself before
> You can ever win a prize
> Life's battles don't always go
> To the stronger or faster man,
> But sooner or later the man who wins
> Is the one who thinks he can.
>
> ANON

Those words certainly gave me some food for thought and I was grateful to Ginny for taking the trouble to put them into my head.

A pat for Ben who is looking decidedly apprehensive about an imminent dressage test.

Taffy and I competed in three events together before someone wanted to buy him and he was sold on. Not long after he left, Crafty was due to run in a three-day event in Sweden. I was delighted to be asked to go on the trip, and this time I didn't make a mess of it.

In July Heather asked me if I wanted to stay on at Ivyleaze.

By now I had been to a world championship and a European championship. What I wanted to do next was groom at the Olympics. To my mind, that would round things off nicely. Heather explained that since Nicks was grooming the advanced horses she would, of course, be invited to groom at any of the major events that came their way. This meant that if I wanted to achieve my Olympic goal I felt I'd have to leave and team up with someone else.

At this point, Fate stepped in and took charge of events. Nicks announced that she wanted to leave after the European championships in Germany, which left Heather without an experienced groom. She offered me the chance to look after the advanced horses and asked if I would like to try my hand at a little secretarial work.

Just then I had some bad news from home. A relative had died, so I went up to Northumberland for a few days to be with the family. While I was away, the Ivyleaze residents had a dramatic encounter with danger. It seems that a spark from an open fire lodged itself under a carpet and burned its way through to the floorboards. The household was awoken at about 5 a.m. to find the rooms full of smoke. Heather shouted to everyone to leave the house, and she removed one of the burning mats herself. They say that there's no smoke without fire, but fortunately in this case it was mostly smoke. When I returned I found that the whole house smelled of burning – even my toothbrush tasted of smoke.

After three months it was obvious to me that I couldn't cope with both the office work and the horses, at least not during the season, so Heather released me from the typewriter and sent me back on the yard.

In 1988, for the first time, I really enjoyed the spring season and the build up of Murphy and Crafty. I had relaxed more, had found a little confidence, could communicate more readily with those around me – and it wasn't long before my Olympic dream was to be fulfilled.

CHAPTER 8

Home and Away

As the season progresses, packing the lorry for shows becomes easier. As far as the horses' tack and clothing are concerned, there is a checklist for each individual. The one for Priceless looked like this:

Dressage bridle
  flash noseband
  rolled reins
  small bridoon bit
Double bridle
Dressage saddle
  white rectangular saddle
    cloth
  white dressage girth marked
    'A'
Jumping saddle
  X noseband
  jumping reins – with
    martingale stops
  French link with cheeks
  Dr Bristol bit
P.'s Stübben saddle
  white Nytack numnah
  blue Cottage Craft girth
  light blue weight-cloth
    numnah
  weight cloth
  46″ cross-country girths
  P.'s surcingle
Martingale
Breastplate with long
  martingale attachment

Cross-country bag
  bandages
  over-reach boots
  tendon protectors
  hind brushing boots
Lungeing cavesson and line
Side reins
Lunge whip
Grooming kit
Stud and plaiting boxes – should
  be in lorry – CHECK
Bandages in vet box – should
  be in lorry – CHECK
Feeds
Hay
Travelling boots (for journey)
Brushing boots
Spare bits
  copper D roller
  rubber gag
  metal gag
  rubber D snaffle
  loose-ring snaffle
Wraps and bandages for after
  the cross-country
Spare cross-country reins,
  girths, etc.

Each horse had a best bridle that was used only for competitions. Sometimes, though, they had to share the odd item, such as a martingale.

The lorry had its own checklist too:

Fill up water tanks
Make sure that Calor gas
    bottles are full
Check oil level in engine
Make sure that generator
    petrol can is full

NEARSIDE OF LORRY
1st cupboard
    1 bag Horsehage
2nd cupboard
    all tack (except saddles) from
        earlier list
    blue box containing spare
        cross-country girths, lead
        for weight cloth, surcingles,
        Cottage Craft girths
    bit tray
3rd cupboard
    selection of 4- and 5-strap
        boots and open-fronted
        boots, various studs, stud
        spanner and tap, scissors,
        plaiting box (check for
        completeness)
    dressage whips and cross-
        country whips
    grooming kit: hoof oil,
        leather punch, spare tail
        bandages, brushes, quarter
        markers, etc.
    vet box: Gamgee, bandages,
        Animalintex, antiseptic
        creams, Fybagee, kaolin,
        wound powder, wound
        wash, cotton wool
    quantity of clean towels

saddle covers
box of Event cubes (for tit-
    bits)
fly spray
disinfectant
tack cleaning kit
wither pads
boot polishing kit
shampoo

OFFSIDE OF LORRY
1st cupboard
    half a bale of hay
    muck sack
    broom
2nd cupboard
    4 buckets
    sponges
    sweat scraper
    muck skip
    small shovel
    feeds

INSIDE LORRY
Selection of coats, Puffas and
    waterproofs
Saddles (on racks)
Lunge whip
Main cupboard
    Dot and Heather's wellies
    Ginny's trainers and
        Muckers
    lorry jack
    liquid paraffin and 60ml
        syringe
    hose pipe

Rug rack
  5 sweat rugs
  5 woollen sponsor's rugs
  1 New Zealand rug
  2 long-neck rain sheets

4 lightweight rein sheets
3 coolers
1 Hansbo rug
2 towelling rugs
1 Thermatex rug

The lorry itself is designed to carry up to six horses, but the most we ever carry is five. The front (spare) partition is usually taken up with saddles and coats.

The only ramp, at the back of the lorry, is on an hydraulic system. At the press of a button the ramp lifts itself slowly into place.

The horses travel at an angle, herringbone fashion, an arrangement with which they all seem comfortable.

The length of the lorry is thirty-six feet, which can cause a few problems when trying to negotiate narrow gateways etc. However, Heather, who undertakes most of the driving, is an expert at tight manoeuvring and always manages to inch the lorry out of trouble. Dot usually copes with the map-reading and travels in the cab next to Heather. Ginny can also drive the lorry but tends to take it on the more routine journeys, such as to the gallops or the hills.

When travelling, the horses have their feeds bagged up for

The Ivyleaze lorry, looking smart and clean after its respray. Notice all the storage cupboards along the side.

the day, placed in buckets and carefully labelled. The teas are stowed beneath the lunches so that the latter can be easily removed first. If ever the horses have to be fed whilst in transit the feeds have to be stored inside the vehicle, otherwise the lorry has to stop to allow someone to retrieve them from the outside cupboard – not a good idea on a motorway as the cupboard is on the traffic side and the lorry is fairly wide.

The horse's hay is placed in Horsehage bags and as usual they are given small portions in hay nets throughout the day.

Ginny usually takes care of her own riding clothes, but it is wise to check that her spurs are on board, as she often wears them for schooling at home.

It is essential not to forget to check that the correct number of waterproofs has been packed. If the heavens open and there aren't enough macs to go round, somehow it often turns out to be me who goes without. I soon learned that it is in my own interest to count the coats.

The contents of the lorry living-area have to be checked, too. The cupboards are stocked with a large selection of tinned foods etc., but the everyday items to check are things such as cornflakes, sugar, coffee, tea and orange squash.

Heather makes a point of overseeing the packing of the foodstuffs, while Dot inspects the equipment for the horses.

If the lorry is away overnight, night rugs and rollers have to go in, as do extra feeds and hay, including the dustbins in which to soak the hay. These take up a fair amount of space but room has to be found for them at the front of the lorry, so that if the horses have to be unloaded quickly the bins won't be in the way. Clip-on mangers are another useful extra – you can never rely on clean mangers being provided elsewhere. The next day's hay has to be weighed out and stored in nets, ready to soak. The feeds also have to be made up in bags; chaff and sugar-beet is added just before feeding.

On arrival at a showground the first items on the agenda are to find the secretary's tent and to locate the dressage and show-jumping arenas and the start of the cross-country.

My first job is to prepare the horses for Ginny or Dot to

work before the dressage. Once they have left I can get on with tidying up the travelling gear (which I put under the ramp if it isn't raining), rolling up the bandages ready for re-use and filling up the water buckets.

I loathe being at competitions in the rain. It is so difficult to keep the horses and the tack looking clean. The comings and goings outside the lorry soon make the ground around it squelchy and slippery. In the end, practically everything gets covered in mud, including me. Moreover, finding room for wet rugs inside the lorry is difficult and makes the inside of the normally spacious box seem small.

The horses always wear studs to compete in, the type depending on the going. Regardless of the conditions underfoot, they all wear small square road studs (never pointed ones) in front for the cross-country.

The horses are bridled inside the lorry so that there is no chance of losing a halterless horse. Also, it gives us more control when unloading them in strange surroundings. If they have to stand outside the lorry for a while, they are tied to string loops fitted to tie-rings. I always try to keep an eye on any youngsters who are tied up, as it is all too easy for them to learn that if they pull, it will give them their freedom.

One horse, Jack, used to be very naughty in this respect. At Newbury one very wet and windy day, Ginny brought him back to the lorry and I emerged from the dryness inside, still struggling to get my arms into my coat sleeves as I climbed down the lorry steps. Jack took one look and, deciding that he was witnessing a close encounter of the third kind, made a fast getaway. He disappeared in the direction of the dressage arena, and I had visions of him galloping through the middle of someone's test. Luckily he was caught before he had the chance.

Another of his little tricks was to chew off the rubber trim along the side of the lorry, which was not a very endearing habit.

When away at competitions, feeding times have to be arranged to suit the horses' riding times. Sometimes we feed half the ration after the dressage, and the rest after the cross-country. At other times it is simpler to wait until the competition is over before feeding.

After a horse has finished his cross-country we always allow him an hour to relax and recover. During this time he is offered a drink and a little hay. Only after that hour is up do we give him a full feed, if he is due for one.

The schedule for a typical day's outing to a one-day event can be fairly hectic. The following is a run-down of one day's activities at Kings Somborne in 1988, where Ginny was riding Murphy, Ben and Crafty. Ben had performed his dressage test the day before, and the horses were accommodated in stabling at Chattis Hill, just over thirty minutes' drive from the event.

A.M.

6.30 Fed horses as usual
Mucked out three boxes
Collected and loaded tack and equipment into lorry
Soaked hay and made up feeds for the day

7.45 Hasty breakfast

8.00 Left Chattis Hill for Kings Somborne

8.45 Arrived at competition

9.10 Ben tacked up for lungeing
Murphy tacked up and taken by me for a walk around showground

9.30 Ben lunged by Dot and afterwards taken for a walk by Heather

9.35 Murphy back at lorry ready for Ginny to work-in for dressage

10.00 Crafty fed in the lorry
Ben returned and put back inside lorry

10.24 Murphy performed his dressage test, videotaped by me
On return to lorry, Murphy reloaded and Ben tacked up for show jumping

Quarter marks add a finishing touch to the horse's turn-out and are usually put on just before the dressage.

11.00 Crafty unloaded and taken for a quiet walk by me

11.08 Ben performs his show jumping
On return to lorry Ben is untacked and fed

11.30 Murphy unloaded and taken for walk (ridden) by me

P.M.

12.00 Ginny warmed up Murphy for show jumping

12.33 Murphy performed his show jumping
Crafty tacked up for dressage

12.45 Murphy returned to lorry, untacked, reloaded and given a small feed
Ginny started working-in Crafty

109

1.12   Crafty performed his dressage

1.30   Crafty returned to box, untacked and reloaded
       Ben prepared for cross-country

2.06   Ben started on cross-country

2.15   Crafty prepared for show jumping
       Ben returned to lorry, untacked, washed down, etc.

2.45   Crafty performed his show jumping

2.50   Crafty returned to lorry and untacked
       Murphy prepared for cross-country

3.36   Murphy set off on cross-country

3.50   Murphy returned to lorry, untacked, washed down,
       etc.

4.45   Crafty prepared for cross-country

5.18   Crafty set off on cross-country

5.30   Crafty returned to lorry, untacked, washed down, etc.
       Ben and Murphy given tea-time feed

6.30   Crafty given tea-time feed
       Hay nets given for journey

7.00   Depart Kings Somborne

9.00   Arrive Ivyleaze
       Unload horses, change rugs etc.
       Set horses fair for night

Of all the many horse trials we have been to up and down the country, one of the ones I enjoy most is Thirlestane Castle. The setting is really beautiful and it is lovely to watch the horses doing their dressage with the castle as the backdrop. The atmosphere is always relaxed and friendly.

In fact, many of the events we have been to are set in picturesque surroundings – Witton Castle and Holker Hall, to name but two. I have to admit that I do have a slight bias

Ben and Ginny taking up water-skiing? Miraculously Ginny managed to survive this near tumble and stayed on board. Kings Somborne, 1988.

towards the North, but many of the southern events were also in delightful locations.

With so very many outings to different destinations it is inevitable that occasionally items are left behind. I have never (so far!) managed to commit the ultimate sin of failing to pack a saddle for an event. I did once leave a cross-country bridle behind, but – as luck would have it – the horse didn't run, so I was spared.

Our worst accident with a horse at a competition was the one involving Ginny and Ben at Smith's Lawn, which I have recounted earlier. That incident taught me the value of having a well-stocked veterinary box at all times. The unfortunate horse suffered a nasty fall which damaged his knees unmercifully. He looked a complete shambles when he got to his feet. While waiting for the vet we washed his knees, taking care

111

to remove every trace of grit and grime (which if left can cause an infection). He was later poulticed and bandaged, and with extreme care loaded into the lorry for the journey home. I travelled with him most of the time and unplaited him as we went along. His forelock had been totally shaved off, as he had scraped his head on the road surface. It is not a day I like to remember.

I do, however, like to recall my lap of honour with Priceless at Locko Park in 1985. Ginny had scooped up first and second places, Night Cap taking the major prize and becoming British National Champion. I didn't have my riding hat with me at the time so Heather whisked me off to a trade stand to borrow one from the shelves. With the price tags and labels tucked inside, and no hair net to tame my wayward curls, I cantered Priceless behind Night Cap – and managed not to overtake!

Grooming at foreign competitions is always interesting, as everything is so different. The atmosphere at events abroad is usually very friendly, which helps one's morale.

On foreign trips we often give another horse a lift, which

Crafty yawns as he waits with Dot at Harwich Docks, on his way home from Sweden in 1987.

means that I have to remember to leave a space for his belongings as well.

Most of our ferry crossings have been relatively calm. On our way back from Sweden in 1987 we decided to give one ferry a miss and to wait for the next, hoping that the weather would improve. When Heather heard the forecast she simply refused to board the ship. We later discoverd what a wise move that had been.

Once on board and battened down for security, the routine is to lower the ramp to allow what little air there is in a ship's hold to circulate to the horses. We try to avoid giving the horses the water supplied by the ferry, as we can never rely on its purity and are anxious to avoid any upsets.

The more stuffy the conditions, the more water we offer the horses so that they don't become dehydrated. On the run-up to a big competition we add glucose to the horses' feed, as not only does it provide extra energy but also we believe that it helps to prevent travel-sickness. Not once on any of my long trips with the horses have they become sick, run a temperature, or sweated up.

Driving a big lorry along foreign roads can have its problems. In Sweden we were happily motoring along a country road, unwittingly heading straight for a low bridge. We had passed a warning sign, but by the time we realised what it meant, it was too late. Instinctively we all ducked as we went under. I think we had just inches to spare.

That wasn't the end of the story, as the Irish rider John Watson, who was driving a high lorry with a roof rack loaded with bales of Horsehage, was following some way behind us. He, too, missed the warning sign, and when he arrived at the competition we all had a good laugh at the ripped Horsehage bags flapping in the breeze.

On a trip to L'Lion d'Angers in France we had great fun losing our way and driving at least twice round the same town. On the same journey we slowed down in the dark to read a sign, which practically gave Dot heart failure – she thought we were heading down a cycle lane in a thirty-six foot lorry!

The trip to Gawler, Australia, for the World Championships in 1986 was quite an experience. I went along as Priceless's official groom and looked after him for the month in which he was in quarantine at Wylye. The German team joined us for the period, as did Mark Todd and Charisma.

The story of the Championships, of Priceless's stunning victory and of the British team's gold medal has already been told in Ginny's book devoted to her champion.

It was great to see how they did things 'Down Under' and to share some of the real camaraderie that exists in the eventing world. As a souvenir, apart from her gold medal, Ginny brought back a jarred shoulder, not acquired when riding the cross-country course but during the wild celebrations after the event! It stayed with her for several months as a painful reminder of a really wonderful party.

CHAPTER 9

Seoul – An Olympic Dream

By the end of July 1988 the Olympics were getting really close and we were preparing to set off for the first team 'concentration' at Badminton. This was to lead up to a final trial at Holker Hall the following weekend. The team selectors had still not made their final choice but they were interested in two of our horses, Ben and Crafty.

The other riders present were Rachel Hunt with Aloaf, Ian Stark with Glenburnie and Sir Wattie, Captain Mark Phillips with Cartier, Karen Straker with Corriwack and Get Smart, Rodney Powell with The Irishman and Special Appointment, Lorna Clarke with Fearliath Mor and Royal Eventer, Ros Bevan with Horton Point and Jane Thelwall with King's Jester.

Team concentrations can be a bit tense since everyone wants his or her horses to go well. Both riders and grooms have to contend with being out of their own environment, and they cannot, for example, turn their horses out to relax them as they would at home. From a groom's point of view, you have to keep a close eye on what is going on all the time. Plans change quite often and you need to know exactly what the riders are doing, where they have to go and where you have to be to meet them.

On Sunday 31 July, the first concentration at Badminton began. We had to be there by 10 a.m. so that the horses could be trotted up before the selectors. I set off from Ivyleaze with Ben and Crafty, both in good spirits, and trotted some of the way there along the road. The horses had already been out

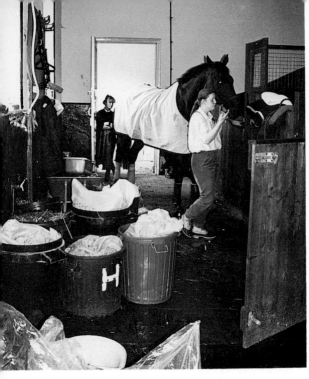

Cartier and his groom, Debbie, in the stables at Badminton. In the foreground are our dustbins full of soaking hay.

for a stretch and a nibble of grass in one of the fields at home, having been turned out at 7 a.m.

I arrived at Badminton, tidied up the horses, and untacked them ready for Ginny to trot them up. I was about to give Crafty to Ginny when she asked me to do the honours because her damaged ankle, which she had sustained by courtesy of Murphy three months ago, was still giving her pain. I'd never done this before and felt quite self-conscious having to run in front of so many eminent people – but of course they weren't looking at me!

In the afternoon, when the horses had settled in to their stables in one of the quiet yards at Badminton House, I took them out for a graze in hand to relax them and give them something to do.

The next day, work started in earnest, with Ginny and the horses having lessons from Pat Manning. Trainers Ferdi Eilberg, Pat Burgess and Jane Holderness-Roddam were also there to help and advise the team. In between the lessons, fittening work went on as usual, mostly in the form of hacking round the Park at Badminton and the surrounding area,

116

and Ginny even found time to take part in an event at Aston Park with some of her novices.

At the end of the week, horses and jockeys had been honed (near) to perfection and we set off for Holker Hall and our stabling at nearby Cartmel racecourse. Unfortunately Heather had to park the lorry quite some distance from the stables and we had to trek backwards and forwards across the racecourse, ferrying all the horses' belongings.

The stables themselves were quite small and stuffy. With the weather so warm, I thought that we should keep a close eye on the horses because these were the hottest conditions that they had been in and it would be interesting to see how they coped, as it would certainly be hot in Seoul.

The next day was sunny and warm. Ginny, never one to miss an opportunity, was competing on no fewer than three horses – Jack, an intermediate, was brought along to make up the trio – so this meant that I was kept pretty busy all day.

Crafty performed well in the dressage, despite the heat. Ben put on a creditable show, too – but in the show jumping he really couldn't be bothered to make the effort and had two fences down, which was disappointing. Crafty went clear, as I thought he would.

After a minor hiccup at the start of the cross-country, when Ginny was about to set off wearing the wrong number, I was able to relax and enjoy their round. From what I could see of the course, Crafty gave Ginny a superb ride and came in looking really fit and not overtaxed by his efforts. Although it was hot, he recovered quickly, which we took as an encouraging sign. I washed him off with cold water and let him graze and relax. I offered him a drink so that he didn't become dehydrated, and tried to keep him in the shade as much as I could.

Just as we were about to start warming up Jack, I noticed that he was quite lame. Close examination of the troublesome leg revealed a small cut on the bulb of his heel. We concluded that he must have stood on a flint and developed a slight infection in the leg. He therefore didn't have his chance to run and I couldn't help feeling guilty that I hadn't noticed the cut the night before. Ginny was quite worn out, having burnt up vast amounts of nervous energy due to the pressures of team selection, so I think she was secretly pleased not to have to go again.

The following morning I was up early to prepare the horses for the final vets' inspection. Once again I had to do the running up, as Ginny's ankle was still giving her trouble.

After breakfast, everyone on the short-list was collected together by the selectors to be told who was going to be chosen for the Olympic team. My heart was in my mouth as I waited: I could hardly dare to keep my ears open. The news that Ginny and I hoped for so much brought a great grin to my face – I couldn't help but be overjoyed, not to say relieved. Both horses would travel to Seoul, with Ben as Ginny's second horse.

The other team members were named as: Mark Phillips on Cartier, Ian Stark on Sir Wattie, and either Lorna Clarke on Fearliath Mor, or Karen Straker on Get Smart. The team reserve wouldn't be known until we got to Seoul, when all the horses would be run up and we would be told which would be scratched. The other two reserves were Rodney Powell with The Irishman or Special Appointment, and Rachel Hunt with Aloaf; their horses would have to go into isolation with the others, at Badminton in a fortnight's time.

The next two weeks were taken up with keeping Crafty and Ben fit and well, but it was 'business as usual' for the other horses. We all tried not to fuss around them unduly but we couldn't help being a little over-protective at times. Ginny did take them out to a couple of events, though not necessarily to tackle the cross-country phase.

On Monday 15 August we took our two hopefuls to Badminton for the obligatory period of isolation.

Despite the looming pressures of the Olympics, this fortnight was fairly leisurely for me, as I was freed of all the usual chores associated with a big yard, and it was pleasant to be able to spend time chatting to the other grooms while grazing the horses in hand or hacking through the Park. Grazing the horses took up most of my spare time and when I wasn't in the stables I could usually be found hanging on to the end of a

The team grooms and their horses line up for the Sponsors' Day photographs at Badminton.

lead rope, horse attached, with my Walkman for company.

We grooms were allowed to use the swimming pool in the grounds of the house, which was good fun, and had our own TV room etc. Accommodation was provided above the stables as usual; the beds were as comfortable as ever.

The horses were hacked out and/or schooled every day, and Ginny had lessons from the various trainers who were helping the team, including Pat Manning, Pat Burgess, and show jumper Nick Skelton. In between times, the boys were given a little freedom in the indoor school for a frolic and a roll, and were grazed in hand whenever the weather permitted. I worked especially hard at their grooming and strapping, trying to ensure that my two horses would gleam under the Korean sun.

All the grooms were given team outfits, contained within a matching suitcase and holdall. The official kit consisted of a blue blazer, grey skirt, two shirts, a tie, shoes and tights. We were also given a tracksuit, trainers, sports socks, and a shiny jacket with matching tracksuit pants and T-shirts. The colours were mostly red, white and blue in various combinations. We had a great time swapping different items until eventually everyone had a wardrobe that vaguely fitted.

On 31 August I had to prepare the horses for a final trot-up in front of the selectors. Dot and Ginny had gone up to London to sort out some of the team kit and hadn't arrived back at the appointed time. Lord Patrick Beresford, the team chef d'équipe, asked me if I would trot the horses up, but I didn't want to do this without a representative of the Holgate team present. Happily, Heather appeared on the scene at the last minute, closely followed by Dot and Ginny, full of apologies for their late arrival. Both horses passed with flying colours.

The next day all the sponsors who had given products to the team came down to Badminton for a Sponsors' Day. The horses were plaited up and polished till they shone. However, it turned out to be a miserable day and the official photographs took ages to arrange because the sessions were constantly interrupted by showers.

The time had come to start planning the packing. Lord Patrick wanted a list of *everything* that was to be taken. This meant that you virtually had to pack the entire trunk to be sure that the list was accurate. The horses had been given several new rugs and it was hard to know where to put them all. Moreover, I had to decide which ones we would need on the flight and which ones could safely be stowed at the bottom of the trunk.

By Monday 5 September, the two reserves – Rachel Hunt and Rodney Powell – had gone home, leaving behind only those travelling to Seoul. It must have been so anti-climactic for them, not to have been included, but they hid their disappointment and departed with cheery good-luck messages for the team. It was sad to see them go.

Having spent a couple of weeks in each other's company, the team members and their grooms had formed quite a close-knit little group, with team spirit and camaraderie obvious for all to see. There were no petty jealousies; no arguments; everyone was working together to support one another. I reflected at the time that although I had accompanied Ginny on many team events abroad, I have never experienced such positive team morale.

I set about preparing the horses' feeds for the journey – we were to leave early the next morning. I carefully weighed out the rations, and stored the meals in separate bags. I set aside two spare buckets for use en route so that we wouldn't be caught out if facilities were limited. As usual, soaked hay was prepared and put into nets.

I toyed with the idea of leaving some of the extra rugs behind, but Heather felt I should take them all. As it turned out, this was sound advice.

In the evening, Crafty was introduced to the Cromovet equipment. This was medicated air vapouriser operated by a foot pump, and was designed to help keep his lungs clear and free from dust. We don't usually employ anything like this, but since the plane was likely to be dry and dusty, we thought it was a sensible precaution.

Later, everyone going to Seoul enjoyed what turned out to be a rather festive supper in the old servants' hall of Badminton House. The Duke and Duchess of Beaufort came to join the riders, and several well-wishers popped in to bid us all good luck. The atmosphere was heady with excitement and anticipation.

The lorry that was taking us to Stansted airport arrived at about 8.30 p.m. A few of us moved its partitions around until we found exactly the arrangement we wanted, while the lorry driver scratched his head and no doubt thought we were quite insane to go to such lengths. Eventually we loaded up most of our gear and called it a day.

I went to bed at about 10.30 p.m. only to be woken three hours later to begin preparations for the journey. I felt as though I had had five minutes' sleep!

I gave the horses a small feed and some hay, and bandaged them up in double Gamgee with Woof travellers on top. Each wore a tail guard attached to a surcingle, with a sweat rug and travelling rug over the top. This arrangement allowed me to change rugs without having to undo tail guards and rollers.

I gave my horses a leg stretch by walking them for about thirty minutes before loading them on to the lorry. At 2.50 a.m. we set off. Dot and Ginny, who would be flying out separately the next day, arrived from Ivyleaze to see us off and to wish us good luck. A small party of riders and staff from Badminton also lost sleep to bid us farewell.

We hadn't gone very far when Royal Eventer, Lorna Clarke's second horse, decided that he didn't like standing, and attempted to sit down in the lorry. Alison, Ian Stark's groom, and I tried to settle him but he was too busy working himself into a frenzy to even notice us. Because the lorry was articulated, there was no access to the cab and, of course, the driver was oblivious to our problems. In desperation Debbie, Mark Phillips' groom, attempted to attract his attention by banging with a shovel. Eventually he pulled up.

By this time, Royal Eventer had gone down and there was nothing we could do to get him up. We decided to undo some of the partitions and lower the back ramp. Throughout, he lay still. We pushed and heaved, then suddenly he got to his feet and walked down the ramp as if nothing had happened. His rump and hips were red and sore from throwing himself against the partitions. We put a few more rugs on him and wondered what to do.

Using the lorry driver's carphone I called Badminton to explain what had happened. Ian Stark answered and said that he would come and find us. Although we were less than ten minutes away, I couldn't say exactly where we were, as it was quite foggy. Worse, I actually told him the wrong road.

Dot and Ginny found us first, then Ian arrived after a detour. It was decided that we should go on without Royal Eventer and that Heather would bring the Holgate lorry to pick him up and would follow on behind, if the horse was all right to travel. In the end his plane ticket was cancelled.

The rest of the journey was uneventful (thank goodness) and we arrived at the airport at about 7.15 a.m.

After checking passports and handing in luggage etc., we were allowed ten to fifteen minutes to walk the horses around before loading them into cargo boxes, which were hoisted on to the plane, a Boeing 747.

At first I was allocated a box with shavings, and had just settled down with all my belongings when I was told I should have been given a box with peat. The ensuing confusion meant that my horses had to be unloaded and all my gear piled up on the tarmac. I had to repack everything in the new cargo box. My two were the last to board the plane.

Each cargo box was partitioned for two horses, although they normally carried three. This meant that I had plenty of room to change rugs etc. There was a chest bar at the front instead of a door, so access was simple.

The plane took off at about 1.20 p.m. Neither Crafty nor Ben had flown before but they behaved impeccably. I stayed with them in their cargo box just in case. A horse's normal reaction on take-off is to sit so far back on his hocks that he loses his front legs. To counteract this I encouraged Ben and Crafty to stand well forward, with their heads over the front bar. Once we were up, they were fine and settled down well.

I tried to persuade them to drink, as dehydration can be quite a problem on long journeys. They soon got the idea and drank well, which was good.

The temperature inside the aircraft was kept down to help

A few of the British grooms 'camping' on the flight out to Seoul.

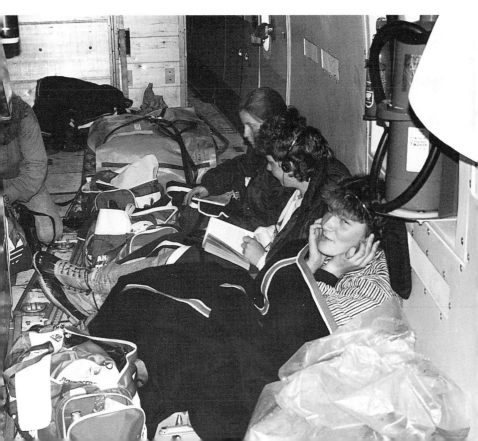

the horses stay cool. I kept a close eye on their temperatures throughout the flight, and adjusted the rugs whenever necessary.

We stopped in Moscow for about an hour, but of course we weren't allowed off the plane. A Russian guard was posted outside the aircraft door to make doubly sure no one got off – or on for that matter.

We had a smooth flight to Seoul, arriving at about 3 p.m. local time. When the doors were opened, hot air rushed in to greet us, confirming our suspicions about the temperatures outside.

We unloaded the horses with the minimum of fuss, walked them around for fifteen minutes on the tarmac, which was burning hot, then put them into a truck which would transport them into quarantine at the Olympic Equestrian Park. I managed to take some water with me and was able to give the horses something to drink while they waited in the lorry. They were both thirsty. When our gear and hand luggage had been checked out we left the airport. After about threequarters of an hour, we arrived at the quarantine stables but couldn't unload until a few formalities had been sorted. All the while, the horses stood patiently in the stuffy lorry and I couldn't help thinking what paragons they both were.

I was pleased to see Malcolm Wallace, the team manager, and Brian Perry, the stable manager, both of whom had arrived a few days earlier. They had organised paper bedding in the boxes and had ensured that a supply of purified water was laid on. (The traveller's saying, 'Don't drink the water' held good for the horses, too.)

All in all, it didn't take long to unload and settle in. The horses were obviously tired, so I attended to them as quickly as I could and left them in peace in their new surroundings.

Having discovered where I was supposed to eat and sleep, I took a cool shower and tumbled into bed.

The next morning I was allowed a bit of a lie-in (until 7.30 a.m.) because of the time change. However, I was woken early by the unexpected trilling of noisy crickets doing their best to raise me from my slumbers.

After the boys had been fed I went for breakfast at the canteen and then tried to tidy up some of the mess and unpack the trunk. I led the horses out for about twenty minutes and let them relax. Ben decided to have a roll. I fed them again at 11.30 a.m. and then left them to their own devices. Like me, they seemed a little jet-lagged.

The next thing to organise was an identity pass, without which my movements would have been very restricted indeed. All the grooms were taken by minibus to the Olympic Village, about twenty-five minutes away, to have our photographs taken and IDs issued.

When I returned to the stables the horses were dozing quietly, so I let them be, and carried on with the unpacking.

Before long, Dot and Ginny arrived and seemed pleased with the horses. They, too, were tired and in need of some sleep. Ginny went off to her room at the Olympic Village and I showed Dot to our room in the Equestrian Park. (Heather was to arrive a couple of days later.)

The next morning we were up with the larks (or should I say the crickets?) to feed and muck out. There wasn't a lot to do, as Ginny decided not to ride, so I took the opportunity to go shopping in Seoul with some of the grooms from the show jumping team. We visited a street market cluttered with rows of little stalls, and quickly learned that it was essential to barter for anything you wanted to buy.

The array of goods on offer was incredible: leather goods and fake Rolex watches being a speciality it seemed. I managed to negotiate a good price for a leather jacket, of all things – much to Dot and Ginny's surprise.

I arrived back at the Equestrian Park at about 6 p.m. Dot had decided to lunge the horses as the evening cooled, and Ginny was there to watch them work.

The horses were released from quarantine on the Friday morning and moved into the barn stabling allocated to the British team. I then set about clipping Crafty, which took me quite some time as his coat is so very fine. In the end I thought he looked respectable.

The next day I clipped Ben, who took exception to the

One of the busy street markets in Seoul.

whole procedure and continued to fidget throughout.

There were still seven days before the Games officially opened, and nine before the three-day event began. We all felt satisfied that the horses were settling in well and adjusting to the climate. In order not to stress them, most of the schooling and hacking was carried out early in the morning, and wherever possible we kept to the routine we had at home.

Ginny was careful to introduce the horses to some of the stranger sights and sounds that Seoul had to offer, such as soldiers patrolling the main stands and a multitude of flags, which Crafty detests at the best of times.

Back at the stables we Brits were taking no chances with security, and a rota was worked out so that we shared guard duty in shifts during the night. I shared mine with Dot and just about managed to stay awake, but goodness only knows what I would have done if an intruder had appeared.

One morning, when Ginny was doing some jumping practice, Ben was behaving rather badly and just not paying attention. He was so careless that he tried to bounce a stride fence and managed to get a pole between his legs, somersaulting himself and Ginny on to the floor. Ginny picked herself up and seemed OK; Ben had grazed his knees, but no serious damage was done. Apparently some rather exaggerated stories about the incident appeared in the British press.

The next morning Ginny felt stiff and sore and the team physiotherapist recommended that she didn't canter, and preferably didn't ride all that day. Crafty needed a canter, so something would have to be done. According to official rules, grooms are only allowed to ride competing horses on a loose rein. Images of me cantering off on Crafty with no reins to stop him flashed through my mind. In the end Ginny did canter Crafty, and Lord Patrick Beresford requested special permission for me to canter Ben who, after all, was Ginny's second horse and unlikely to compete. I was allowed to ride and canter twice, which we both really enjoyed.

The evenings were pretty quiet and warm, and since there wasn't any entertainment I spent most of them chatting to other grooms and competitors and sipping cold drinks from the canteen. A trip into town was a major expedition since there were no buses and taxi fares could be extortionate. I knew quite a number of the foreign grooms, especially those who were based in Britain, like Mark Todd's grooms Helen and Debbie, and David Green's groom, Claire.

Ginny recovered from her fall quite quickly and was soon back in action. One day she thought she'd try out the cross-country practice fences which the Koreans had built, but found that they had been put up in an area the size of a postage stamp. Since they weren't demanding in size or complexity she didn't bother to put Crafty over them but gave Ben a run for his money, just for fun. He, of course, was overjoyed.

By now, Ben had worked out that he could duck beneath the chain across his stable doorway. The sliding stable doors had bars at the top which prevented the horses from looking out, and since the stables were fairly small, opening the doors and putting a chain across instead gave them a little extra room to move around. I managed to put a stop to his little game by hanging a rug over the chain, but not before he had walked out twice! He also discovered that he could nip the other horses as they were taken in and out. Of course, I disowned him.

Crafty, likewise, was getting a little above himself and took great delight in tormenting his next-door neighbour, Cartier. He also amused himself by systematically removing all the rugs on the rack outside his stable whenever he thought no one was looking.

On 17 September the official opening ceremony took place and I looked after the horses until Ginny and the other competitors came to ride in the afternoon. Ginny decided to jump them both and was pleased to find that neither sweated up badly, even though it was hot.

The next day, the horses had to be presented for the vets' inspection. Ben got quite excited about being plaited up, and I hadn't the heart to tell him that this was probably going to be his only official outing. I, on the other hand, didn't get excited about wearing my uniform as I disliked the shiny tracksuit pants, but I suppose they didn't look too bad with the team T-shirt.

Ben went first and was passed. Crafty, however, was trotted up twice, which was a little nerve-racking. We knew that there was nothing wrong with him but as Ginny turned to trot back she was a bit left behind because she still couldn't run too well on her injured leg. One more trot-up and he passed as sound. (Sighs of relief all round.)

All the other horses presented were passed but unfortunately Lorna had to be left out of the team because Fearliath Mor had knocked himself a few days before and had a little heat in his leg. Everyone knew how desperately disappointing this was for Lorna, but she showed her true character by remaining totally supportive of the other team members throughout the Games.

On the 19th, while Ginny went up to Wondang to walk the cross-country course, I rode Crafty up to the main dressage arena to watch Captain Mark Phillips and Cartier do their test, and to show Crafty a few more flags at the same time. While Cartier was in the arena the heavens opened (and I mean really opened) and we were all drenched, including the Captain who rode extremely well considering that his saddle was soaked and slithery. By the time Cartier had finished his test, the place was deserted – and no wonder.

The following day I prepared Crafty for his dressage test, which was to be ridden at 8 a.m. I was up at 4.30 (before the crickets) and Ginny stayed in my room so that she wouldn't have to travel over from the Olympic Village in the morning. Everything was ready by 7 o'clock, allowing Ginny to potter off for a 30-minute hack before returning to the arena for a more serious warm-up.

Dot and Ferdi were both there to keep an eye on her and to make sure that Crafty was working well. In fact he performed very calmly in his test and earned himself a pretty good mark. He was lying third, with Mark Todd and Charisma in first place, and the German rider Claus Erhorn on the former British event horse, Justin Thyme, in second.

I told him what a good boy he was and took him back to the stables, where I had to make ready for our removal to Wondang for the cross-country phase. A whole convoy of trucks left the Equestrian Park with a police escort at 2.30 p.m. and arrived at its destination about two hours later. (During our absence I had arranged for Ben to be looked after by Nick Skelton's groom, Mark Beaver.)

Once again we had been allocated stables in a barn, and these were fairly large and airy. Unfortunately there was no purified water for us when we arrived, so the horses had to make do with small drinks from our travelling containers until the engineer had fitted up the equipment in the evening.

In order to prevent anyone snooping round the stables or

Dot and Ginny discuss Crafty's dressage performance while I tell him what a good boy he was.

interfering with the horses it was decided that I should sleep in front of the sliding doors next to Crafty's box. Other grooms were sleeping in a temporary dormitory in the barn so I wasn't entirely alone.

I fed Crafty at about 5 a.m. Everything was handy: I just pulled myself out of bed, wandered over to him in my nightie, gave him his breakfast and went back to bed. I gave him his second feed at 8 o'clock, mucked out, then started to prepare the equipment for the steeplechase and the ten-minute halt. It looked to me as though I didn't have enough kit – there were no Puffas, raincoats, woolly rugs, New Zealands, etc. – and I asked Dot if she wanted to go through it with me. Dot raised her eyebrows and said, 'Elaine, you've done enough packing over the last few weeks. If you're happy, so am I,' – and that was her last word on the subject.

I pulled the whole lot out (twice) to satisfy myself that I had everything I needed. I definitely hadn't forgotten anything.

Mark Phillips' groom, Debbie, asked if she could borrow the spare bridle that I had made up as a gag at Ginny's request. She said she wanted a rubber gag on the bridle in the ten-minute halt box, just in case it was needed. This was obviously important, so I lent it to her.

Sadly, Cartier had pulled up lame with a painful muscle after Phase C and a forlorn and upset Debbie brought him back to the stables. Not surprisingly she had forgotton about my bridle and had left it with Lorna Clarke at the ten-minute halt box. This wasn't much good to me because if anything happened after the steeplechase, I wouldn't have a spare bridle. Somehow I was going to have to get it back.

It was almost time for Crafty to set off on Phase A, which he did about 11.38. He looked in absolutely tip-top form as I watched him start his first roads and tracks. Fortunately Dot organised the return of the bridle so that I could take it to the steeplechase.

Crafty finished the steeplechase with ease and came into the 'dead area' where his back-up team was allowed to check him and where he could halt for a few moments. Dot, Heather, Uncle Jack and I were in attendance. We quickly sponged him down between his back legs, where the main arteries are, and down his flanks, and we handed Ginny a bag of ice, which she rubbed down his neck – and held on his poll the whole way round Phase C. Afterwards she said that having to stretch forward up his neck and hold the ice between his ears had given her a really bad backache. Nevertheless, she had hoped it would be worth the effort and tried her best to ignore the pain.

We moved to the ten-minute halt box and waited for Ginny to come in from Phase C. She seemed to be taking for ever.

Eventually she arrived, and Crafty was quickly trotted up for the vets. I then took him to a small covered area that offered a little shade. Here two large portable fans were set up, one on each side, to blow cool air on to him. We sponged down his neck, in between his back legs and his flanks. We raised the saddle, but didn't actually wash underneath it. Instead we rubbed the area really hard with a towel to remove the sweat and restore the circulation. His girths were loosened while he rested. I also undid his noseband and Heather gave him a glucose drink. I rubbed his ears and kept an ice-pack on his head for as long as he would allow. Other ice-packs were rubbed on his body to help cool him down.

Alex Chalmers, the team farrier, checked Crafty's shoes and studs. Soon he would be ready for the off.

At a given signal Ginny got back on board – she likes to remount five minutes before she is due to start. By this time I had applied grease to the fronts of his forearms, knees and leg protectors, and to his hind legs from stifle to coronet band. If he hit anything the grease would help him slide over it.

Just as Ginny remounted she turned to Dot and asked her where her other spurs were. Apparently she wanted to change them.

'What spurs?', said Dot, somewhat perplexed.

At this late stage, Ginny, it seemed, wanted her blunt spurs. I said that I hadn't been asked to bring any other spurs, and the curved, blunt spurs that Ginny wanted were nowhere to be seen. I leapt into action, running all the way back to the stables to find them. The worst part was running back up the steep hill to the box, but I made it.

Then Crafty was given an unexpected bonus when his departure was delayed due to a fallen rider on the course. Ginny got off and I led Crafty round; in the end, he had an extra three or four minutes' recovery time before he went across country.

I gathered up our belongings and dashed off to find a monitor so that I could watch Ginny's round. Before I could get there I heard a gasp from the crowd and thought, 'Oh no, she's come off.' In fact she had had a really sticky moment at the fourth fence, a largish jump with a big drop. Crafty had hit the fence with his knees. How Ginny stayed on board I'll never know. If she hadn't slipped the reins as she did, she would have been pulled straight over his head.

I stood and watched the rest of her stunning cross-country round until about fence 20, Crafty jumping boldly and seemingly relishing the task. I picked up my kit and made my way to the finish in readiness.

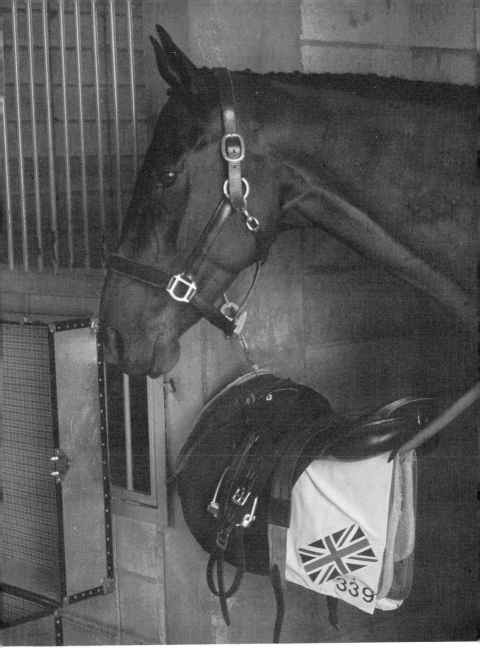

Crafty waiting to be tacked up on cross-country day at Seoul.

Over the loud speakers I could hear that they were approaching and it was really good to see them coming up the hill towards me.

As Ginny pulled up, Crafty breathing hard, I heard her gasp, 'I'm glad that's over'. In between puffing and panting she was patting him as if it were going out of fashion. I hovered in the background waiting for one of the officials to give me the OK to take the horse. A voice shouted, 'Where's the groom?', and having made sure that I could, indeed, take Crafty without contravening the rules, I set about making him more comfortable.

I gave him a big hug, undid his noseband and loosened his girth. Suddenly I remembered Ginny's favourite stick, which as usual she had dropped somewhere near the finish. Luckily I spotted it straightaway.

I walked Crafty quietly back to the stables. He was still blowing quite hard. John McEwen, one of the team vets, walked back with me to the medical box where he could check Crafty over. His temperature was 105°C, which was to be expected. I walked him around for a while then washed him off. I took him for another walk and hosed him down again. By this time (some forty minutes in all) his temperature had dropped back down to normal and he was comfortable. I offered him water frequently but only allowed him small sips at a time.

I allowed him a few mouthfuls of hay before tackling the job of removing the grease on his legs and generally tidying him up. I poulticed his lower legs and knees and left him in his box to rest.

Ginny popped in a few times to see how Crafty was and to offload some of her gear, which I was to look after.

Crafty was walked for about five minutes every hour, to help prevent any stiffening. He had his feeds at normal times and seemed to be fine. He was trotted up in front of the British vets and didn't look too bad. In fact all the horses who had completed the course looked all right.

We trotted Crafty up at 9.30 p.m. and found him a little stiff behind. I walked him for a while to loosen him up, and repeated the exercise a little later that night. The poultices were removed and his legs checked. There were no signs of any swelling, even on his knees. Ann Scott Dunn, our equine therapist, gave him some Faradic treatment after which we left him in peace.

I realised then that I hadn't eaten anything since breakfast. The British Horse Trials Support Group were thoughtful enough to bring sandwiches down to the stables. I was pretty thirsty and helped myself to a bottle of mineral water. I took a big mouthful, only to discover that it was neat vodka! I couldn't help wondering who had needed Dutch courage up at the ten-minute halt box.

That night I slept like a log.

At 5 a.m. Crafty was trotted up and found to be just a touch stiff behind. I walked him round for thirty minutes then gave him his breakfast. Ginny arrived at 7 o'clock and took him for a ride for forty minutes. When she returned she told me he had been quite fresh. He was obviously feeling well.

The official vets' inspection was at 8 a.m. I was rather nervous and didn't want to watch. After running up twice, he passed.

We then had to pack all our goods and chattels and return to the Equestrian Park for the show jumping. A police escort ensured a smooth journey for the convoy of sixteen or so articulated lorries.

After three good rounds on the cross-country (from Ian, Ginny and Karen) our team was still in the hunt for a medal. The Germans looked set to take the gold, and we would have to battle against the Kiwis for silver or bronze. In the individual medal stakes Ginny was lying second overall. Mark Todd on the indomitable Charisma were way out in front, with Ian Stark and Sir Wattie lying third to Ginny.

The show jumping was to prove something of a cliff-hanger.

Some last-minute advice from Nick Skelton helped build Ginny's confidence. In the practice arena Crafty was jumping fluently and didn't hit a single pole. When Ginny went into

Crafty arriving back at the Equestrian Park the day after the cross-country.

the main ring I rushed to the rails to watch and held my breath.

On seeing the crowd, Crafty became mesmerised. His head went up and I could see he wasn't paying attention to Ginny. She guided him round the colourful course as best she could, but couldn't help collecting ten faults as she did so.

Ginny looked disappointed as she left the arena, thinking she had blown the team's chances of a medal. Heather told Crafty he was a naughty boy.

As it turned out, one of the New Zealand team had had five fences down, so, what with Karen Straker's clear round, we were still in the running – but we didn't know it at the time.

Ian went in next and, with a fluent clear round, earned himself an individual silver. Britain clinched the team silver.

Charisma, last to go, rose to the occasion. It was his swan song; he showed the world that he was still the best and, to tumultuous applause, claimed an individual gold for Mark Todd.

It wasn't until the final results were flashed up on the main scoreboard that we realised Ginny had won the individual bronze. We were all so thrilled we couldn't wipe the smiles off our faces.

As for team honours, the Germans won the gold, Britain took the silver and the New Zealanders collected the bronze.

Just as the medal ceremony was about to take place we realised that none of the British grooms was wearing a team tracksuit. Worse, we were sporting such a variety of colours that we looked like a selection of liquorice all-sorts. Someone was despatched at speed to fetch the right clothing, and we were still pulling on the tracksuits as we walked into the main arena.

Once the medal ceremony was over I took Crafty back to the stables for his dope test. I then settled him in his box and let him unwind.

At this point celebrations began in earnest, first at the British Horse Trials Support Group party, then at the Kiwis' do at their stables. Everyone was in high spirits and having the time of their lives.

The next morning I was up and about at 7 a.m. and had fed and mucked out Ben and Crafty before anyone else had stirred. Hangovers were the order of the day for most people.

Over the next ten days before departure, life was much more relaxed. Tensions visibly eased and I could get on with tending the horses in a more normal fashion. I even had the opportunity to enjoy some of the other events taking place at the Games.

It wasn't until we arrived home to the chill of Britain's autumn that I really had the chance to reflect on the excitement of the last month or so. Being part of an Olympic team, though in a minor role, had been an incredible experience. It is the stuff of which dreams are made, and I shall never forget it.

Once back at Ivyleaze, I took great pleasure in turning Ben and Crafty out into the green fields that they had missed for so long. It was lovely to see them trotting round, glad to have their freedom at last, and it was hard to believe that they had come half-way round the world the day before.

As for me, I could have slept for a week.

The end of a perfect Badminton. Ginny and I, proud and happy, meet the Press with Crafty, our newly crowned Badminton champion.

Postscript

In the autumn of 1988 I had been with the Ivyleaze yard for five seasons, and I felt it was time to move on. I decided to leave after the Seoul Olympics. The parting was an amicable one and I knew the door was always open for my return.

I had planned to freelance for a while then to travel, as I had been bitten by the bug and wanted to see more of the world. There didn't seem to be much work on offer around my home town, so as a stop-gap I took a full-time job preparing hunters. Whilst it was enjoyable running a yard in my own way and putting into practice so much of what I had learned at Ivyleaze, I must admit that I missed the hurly-burly of a big competition yard.

Meanwhile my own horse was coming on nicely, and I tried to fit in his schooling before going to work. It was satisfying that we won an unaffiliated event together, at only the third show we attended. It was good to know that the time and effort invested in my training had not been wasted. This was, after all, my first chance to test out the Ivyleaze methods of training and fittening and to see the results for myself.

As the hunting season drew to a close so did my contract. Ginny had asked me to groom Crafty and Ben for her at Badminton, which gave me something to look forward to. About ten days before I was due to travel down to Avon, Ginny rang again, asking me to consider going back to work in her yard.

Badminton 1989 couldn't have been more welcoming. Crafty, the leggy four-year-old who had started his career at the same time as me, had matured into a top-class event horse. I had watched him grow and had helped with his training along the way. Now he was the Whitbread Champion for 1989; the training methods and teamwork had paid off yet again.

It felt good to be back at work.

Index

Figures in *italics* refer to illustrations

141